FIX THIS NEXT

ALSO BY MIKE MICHALOWICZ

The Toilet Paper Entrepreneur

The Pumpkin Plan

Profit First

Surge

Clockwork

MIKE MICHALOWICZ

FIX THIS NEXT

**MAKE THE VITAL CHANGE THAT WILL
LEVEL UP YOUR BUSINESS**

PORTFOLIO / PENGUIN

PORTFOLIO / PENGUIN

An imprint of Penguin Random House LLC

penguinrandomhouse.com

Copyright © 2020 by Mike Michalowicz

Penguin supports copyright. Copyright fuels creativity, encourages diverse voices, promotes free speech, and creates a vibrant culture. Thank you for buying an authorized edition of this book and for complying with copyright laws by not reproducing, scanning, or distributing any part of it in any form without permission. You are supporting writers and allowing Penguin to continue to publish books for every reader.

Most Portfolio books are available at a discount when purchased in quantity for sales promotions or corporate use. Special editions, which include personalized covers, excerpts, and corporate imprints, can be created when purchased in large quantities. For more information, please call (212) 572-2232 or e-mail specialmarkets@penguinrandomhouse.com. Your local bookstore can also assist with discounted bulk purchases using the Penguin Random House corporate Business-to-Business program. For assistance in locating a participating retailer, e-mail B2B@penguinrandomhouse.com.

Library of Congress Cataloging-in-Publication Data
Name: Michalowicz, Mike, author.
Title: Fix this next: make the vital change that will
level up your business / Mike Michalowicz.
Description: New York: Portfolio/Penguin [2020]
Identifiers: LCCN 2019046357 (print) | LCCN 2019046358 (ebook) |
ISBN 9780593084410 (hardcover) | ISBN 9780593084427 (ebook)
Subjects: LCSH: Problem solving. | Organizational change. |
Strategic planning.
Classification: LCC HD30.29 .M53 2020 (print) | LCC HD30.29 (ebook) |
DDC 658.4/06—dc23
LC record available at https://lccn.loc.gov/2019046357
LC ebook record available at https://lccn.loc.gov/2019046358

Printed in the United States of America
3 5 7 9 10 8 6 4 2

BOOK DESIGN BY TANYA MAIBORODA

While the author has made every effort to provide accurate telephone numbers, internet addresses, and other contact information at the time of publication, neither the publisher nor the author assumes any responsibility for errors, or for changes that occur after publication. Further, the publisher does not have any control over and does not assume any responsibility for author or third-party websites or their content.

▼

Business owners are superheroes.

You serve our world, after all.

This book is dedicated to you, superhero.

CONTENTS

As a reader of this book, you can get the book resources
and the Fix This Next evaluation tool for free at
FixThisNext.com

INTRODUCTION

"I OWE YOU A BEER!"

The subject line of Dave Rinn's email caught my attention. I read on.

"I was just sitting here buried. I recently lost one staff member to a lateral move and another is in Hawaii. Instead of three of us carrying the load, I was here alone, crushed under it. We used to just do everything that came our way, but with two people out, it was clear that our approach of putting equal importance on everything wasn't working. We need to do the right things, not everything. Yet I was feeling paralyzed by the multitude of choices. It was like trying to go down every path at once. I didn't know what to do next."

Sitting here buried. Feeling paralyzed. Don't know what to do next. Yup. That sounds about right. Some business owners feel this way from time to time. Most business owners feel this way all the time. That relentless weight of being buried by all of the problems that need to be fixed affects business owners of every level of experience and success. Whether you just started out or your company is the industry leader, whether you've struggled to make payroll or are rolling in profit, that urgent need to fix everything, like now, can cause you to freeze up. Which problem should you tackle first?

Dave runs a successful coaching and cash-management firm. Most days, his solution to overwhelm was an instinctual response: get more people doing more things. Yet when he was down two staff members, he was blessed with the new awareness that not everything is of equal importance. Suddenly, he was dealing with all aspects of his business: intakes, bookkeeping, scheduling coaching calls, making the coaching calls, chasing down data from clients—everything. Down two employees, weak links that were always present were amplified and became crises.

So, why did Dave say he owed me a beer?

"I have always just gone with my gut in the past. I believed that every problem was a problem to be addressed. Every opportunity was an opportunity to be exploited," Dave explained in a follow-up phone call. "In moments like these, I would have just gone into 'fire-extinguisher' mode and put out the fires that were burning my ass. I would have responded to whoever screamed the loudest. And when the team returned, I would switch from 'fire-extinguisher' mode to 'emergency-dispatcher' mode. We had the same problems, except now I told my team which fires to put out. Beholden to the never-ending stream of urgent issues, we had no specific pathway to growth."

But now Dave had a secret weapon. A simple tool, not in his toolbox, but printed out and taped to his wall.

"This time, though, I looked over at my wall and saw the tool you gave me last time we met. It reminded me to slow down, step outside instinct, and ask, 'Okay, instead of doing little bits of everything, what is the one thing I should fix next to move the business forward?'"

The tool taped to Dave's wall is something I call the Fix This Next (FTN) analysis, and I'd given it to Dave as part of a beta-testing group years back. Using it, Dave discovered that he had four issues related to his current problem—two related to sales and client commitments, and two related to overall efficiency, what I call order. In just minutes, he was able to figure out which problem he had to fix next in order to make progress that sticks, and how to approach it. He quickly identified solutions for handling the systems problem: adjust client commitments and adjust his company's workflow.

Dave told me, "Just thinking through it was a calming process. I was no longer spinning out of control. I thought, 'I can handle this. Now I have a pathway.' It pulled me out of my sense of drowning, and I was able to pause and consider what we were missing and what we could address to fix it.

"The fix I came up with wasn't just for the moment," Dave continued. "It was a realignment of the business so that I could straighten out and not have to go into that buried mode over and over again. The fix helped me now and it will help me next year. I am able to address my business's current issues in a way that will serve my company's future. Now, when I find myself questioning what to do, I pause momentarily, evaluate what to address with the FTN analysis, and then find myself back in control and my business moving forward."

When entrepreneurs reach out to me, it's typically to ask for help to make a big change or solve a big problem. Some have hit a sales plateau and no matter what they try, they can't level up. Or they can't dig themselves out of a financial hole. Maybe you have some of the same problems with your business. Maybe you're fully staffed and still dog-tired. Or you've lost your passion for the business because you're not seeing the impact you hoped to make. Or maybe you're looking for a way to leave your mark for generations to come, but don't know how to make it a reality. Whether you are in crisis mode, simply want to grow your business, or want to make a lasting impact on our planet, *Fix This Next* finds the critical issue you need to resolve—wait for it—next! When you are in "fire-extinguisher mode," FTN gives you the pause necessary to pinpoint the core issue. When things are moving along but just not moving forward, FTN points to your true north.

I had taught the system to hundreds of entrepreneurs already and coached many through it. I knew it worked in the lab, but this was the first email I received about how FTN worked "in the wild"—without my prompting or advice. To hear that the tool I developed and tested on my own business over the years actually worked for another entrepreneur made my day. (I owe *you* a beer, Dave.) To learn from hundreds of others, as I would over the coming months, that the system worked for both short-term panic and long-term growth strategies made my whole year. And to hear that a single piece of paper could hang next to your desk, as it does mine, and give you total control of your business . . . that, my friend—*that*—may have made my whole life.

Whether it's staffing issues, or trying to make payroll, or capriciously declaring a goal of more sales, or more efficiency, or more profit, or all of it at once, most entrepreneurs busy their days dealing with the apparent issues. We know we have core challenges that need addressing and problems that need fixing, but we aren't sure which one to focus on first, so we go for the low-hanging fruit. We look at the most obvious thing that seemingly needs to be handled immediately and tell ourselves that we will work on "all the other stuff" later. You know, when we have more time. (You can probably sense my sarcasm, even from outer space.)

Since I have written five books prior to this one, each one dealing with a different core business challenge, the question I am asked most often by entrepreneurs is "Mike, which book should I read first?" A good question, to which I used to give a poor response. I used to say, "You've got to read *Clockwork*." Or whichever book my notable bias thought apropos. My responses were not based on what served my reader nearly as much as what I was most hyped up on at the moment. You know—the apparent.

Now I answer that question with a question. When people ask "What book should I read now?" I respond by asking "What problem in your business do you need to fix next?" If you need to increase sales and grow your client base, then I believe you will find *The Pumpkin Plan** provides a proven strategy to do just that. I am blessed that every day I hear of another business that has "pumpkin planned" healthy growth to great effect. If your sales are sustainable yet you're still struggling to put money in your pocket, then I

---

*Visit PumpkinPlanYourBiz.com to get free resources and access to certified Pumpkin Plan coaches.

humbly submit *Profit First** should be your next read. I am proud, honored, and humbled all at once to say that hundreds of thousands of entrepreneurs have profitable businesses now because they followed the methods detailed in that book. And if you're still chained to your desk wondering when you'll ever get off the hamster wheel that is your business and finally get back to doing the work you love best, then *Clockwork†* is your best bet. Entrepreneurs all over the world—including me—are designing their business to run itself—and taking annual four-week vacations—because they are following the systems I shared in that book. If your struggle is with hiring, leadership, sales techniques, or one of dozens of other common challenges, the solution is out there in one of the many extraordinary books written by my contemporaries.

Still, the question remains. What is the next problem you must fix? The answer to that simple question is of critical importance, but few entrepreneurs know how to answer it. Of all the challenges we face, we aren't sure which one is the most important *right now*. It's a serious concern. How can you be sure which problem or opportunity you need to address first, when you have so many issues on your list? If you are focused on the apparent, you would choose the issue that seems make or break in the moment. Makes sense, right? You know what that issue is because your gut tells you so, or because you are emotionally connected to the outcome, or because it's the easiest issue for you to deal with.

Here's where you would expect me to tell you which challenge

---

*Go to ProfitFirstProfessionals.com to get free resources and to request the services of a certified Profit First expert.
†You guessed it! Free resources and expert help can be found at RunLikeClockwork.com.

to focus on first. (As I'll explain later, it isn't necessarily profit, even though my book *Profit First* may have you thinking otherwise.) Except that I don't know what it is. Honestly, I don't think you know what it is either.

That's why I developed a tool to find the biggest challenges and opportunities in any business quickly, and at any given moment. I'd been following the principles for years, and my books reflected that, but I hadn't yet figured out how to break it all down for other entrepreneurs.

The tool I created gets you out of guessing mode and into fast, impactful, deliberate action. It took me the better part of three years to perfect it, testing it out in my own business and with other entrepreneurs through multiple iterations. Now all you have to do is understand it and follow a 4-step process. Seriously, it's so easy, it can be done in less than fifteen minutes. (And yes, I have a story about that in this book.) The tool is so simple that by chapter 3 you will have mastered the basics and you'll be ready to use it daily. In fact, if you download the tool right now (at FixThisNext.com), you can pin it above your desk and refer to it whenever the need arises—just as Dave did. I hope it becomes your bestest friend, the consigliere who whispers in your ear before you make a critical decision.

Why is the Fix This Next tool so effective? It works because, rather than connect to your gut or emotions, it connects to your business needs—the foundational needs that all businesses have, regardless of size or industry—and provides an order in which to deal with them. When we address the apparent, we may be overlooking a vital need that needs fixing *first*. In solving that need, the apparent issues and other not-so-apparent issues may automatically be resolved.

Think of it like this: You build a house from the ground up. You first need a strong foundation, then a strong first floor, and then upon that a strong second floor, and so on. If you don't consider what supports what, in what sequence, the structure will collapse on itself. The same is true for your business. Focusing on the apparent is similar to replacing windows on the third floor while the basement is in danger of crumbling due to widening cracks in the foundation.

In every book I've ever written, my primary goal has been to simplify some aspect of entrepreneurship so that you can easily use the systems and strategies I present to meet your business goals. Countless entrepreneurs have shared with me the transformation their business experienced after applying one or more of the tools in my earlier books. But this book? This book has the mother of all tools, in my (clearly) not-so-humble opinion.

Now when people ask me which of my books to read first, I have the easiest answer yet. *This book*. Start with *Fix This Next*.

How much time have I spent putting out fires and randomly declaring objectives for my business? Before I started following the principles on which the Fix This Next tool is based, pretty much all of my time was spent on the apparent. Once I figured out how to pinpoint what to focus on next, my businesses grew faster and healthier. Since creating the tool, I've stopped relying on my instinct alone and have started using this system to listen and respond to my company's true needs. Most importantly, I'm committed to empowering you, my friend, so that you never miss another opportunity either. I hope this book is a resource you will refer to over and over again, because the tool never stops working. You can always return to it to pinpoint your biggest challenge, fix it next, and then pinpoint the next one after that as you build your beautiful business, floor by floor. And who knows, maybe one day I'll owe you a beer* too.

Business success is a journey, something you need to navigate for the perpetuity of your company. I am convinced the tool you are about to discover will be your ultimate guide. I also realize that leafing through a couple of hundred pages or listening to hours of audio to revisit the tool each time may not be the best use of your time. So I created a collection of resources for quick reference. You will find a one sheet explaining the tool, the most current (and regularly enhanced) online evaluation, access to certified coaches using *Fix This Next*, and more. It's all free and available now at FixThisNext.com.

You are much closer to your goals than you think you are. You just need to move in the right direction. Let this book be your compass.

---

*I am totally up for a tequila gimlet or an old-fashioned, if you prefer.

FIX THIS NEXT

Chapter 1

THE BUSINESS OWNER'S COMPASS

YOU ARRIVE AT YOUR DESK IN THE MORNING, PUT ON YOUR firefighter gear (your glasses, your email app, and a cup of coffee with a double shot of espresso), and get to work putting out fires. Calm the pissed-off customer. Send out the late proposal. Scramble to cover payroll—right after you deliver a speech to your employees about your company's "bright future." All the while tightly crossing your legs from that third cup of coffee, because who has time to go to the bathroom? #amIright?

Even when you do find time to hunker down with that big project you've been putting off, the question that begs to be answered is, "Does it really matter?" That one big thing you are finally about to tackle, will it really have a significant impact?

For well over a decade, it seemed the fires I put out most were related to a lack of cash. I had a maxed-out megaloan, crazy credit card debt, a house that was refinanced yet again to cover payroll, and a constant feeling of compression in my chest, as though I were having a continuous heart attack, hour after hour, day after day, and month after month. I had to borrow from friends to pay the company's rent, while uncomfortably saying—and pseudo believing—it was an investment in our growth. I let my credit card statements sit on my desk unopened in fear of seeing how much I owed, opening them only when the collection calls came. My credit card debt had surpassed seventy-five thousand dollars . . . and that did not include personal or business loans.

In my hopeless state, I focused on the very apparent solution: sales. I did everything I could to sell more things to more customers. Admittedly, I tried to sell anything to anybody. While more revenue was an obvious solution, as the sales volume improved, profit did not. In fact, as my company made more money, I inexplicably accumulated even more debt, and officially maxed out all sources of loans, putting me at $365,000 in *personal* debt. Yeah, my business "made" more money, while I dug my financial grave. What the hell was going on? Why didn't the increase in sales fix my business? It made no sense to me whatsoever.

If you are familiar with my other books, you may already be familiar with my story and know I eventually realized that more sales alone does not help a business; it actually hurts it. The story I haven't told before is how I came to understand that I had to look for the solution at a different level.

It was in the depths of my desperation that I met a moment of inspiration. One fateful morning, my printer jammed, and I just couldn't get it to work. I pulled out the tray and the toner, opened every flap, and then put everything back the way it was. Still jammed. Then I tried that "fix" again. Pull out the tray and toner, open every flap, then put it all back. Still nothing. I tried the same sequence of steps yet again, just much harder. I yanked open the tray and slammed it back in. I tugged out the toner, shook it like a can of spray paint, and threw it back in. I swung open all those stupid flaps and slapped them back closed. I did this a fourth and fifth time, with growing force and frustration (and perhaps a curse word or two), until I realized that I was instinctually repeating the same fruitless steps over and over, and that I needed to try something different next. Instead of picking the printer up and throwing it out the window, which I was highly tempted to do, I paused and pondered. Since what I was doing wasn't working and, with the force I was using, probably making things worse—what else could it be?

I poked around the back and found a tiny piece of crumpled-up paper caught in the feed. I removed the blockage with a combination of scissors, a paper clip, and masterful hand yoga, and we were back in business. Cue the epiphany! I realized that if the approach I'm using to fix a problem doesn't work, despite repeated attempts and despite my gut instinct to do the same thing but harder, it's not the solution. Right then and there I asked myself, what if my company's problem didn't reside with the sales side of my business but was jammed up in another part? Rather than reverting to "sell more—sell harder," I paused and pondered where my business blockage really was.

I was able to figure out that the apparent sales issue I had was not a sales issue at all. I had a profit issue. All my work to bring in new sales wasn't going to get the job done because I had been working on the wrong problem. The steps I took next all came out of this realization, and wound up saving me and my business.

Applying the solution I came up with, my business became permanently profitable, practically overnight. As of this book's publication date, it has had forty-five (yes, forty-friggin'-five) consecutive quarters of profit distributions—*to me*, the business owner. That solution was the foundation of Profit First, which has helped hundreds of thousands of businesses become profitable.

The funny thing is, the solution of taking the profit first for my business is perhaps unique in its simplicity, but I'm sure I wasn't the first to think of it. I suspect you've probably thought of similar ideas. It's not about coming up with the solution; you already have it in your mind, or someone has written a book on it. The trick is in the timing. Applying the right fix at the wrong time yields a little bit of benefit and a lot a bit of frustration. The key is to apply the right fix at the right time in your company's evolution. The key is to know what to do next.

Over the last twelve years, I've devoted myself to the study of business and entrepreneurship, and I lived it for almost three decades. I've come to understand that all business owners struggle, at every level. Very few achieve their big plans for revenue or for changing the world, let alone turning a profit. And the few that do still seem to end up losing their way at some point. This is not due to a lack of experience or resources, or even money—the three most commonly reported reasons why businesses fail. The biggest problem business owners have is that they don't know what their biggest problem is. Let me say that one more time for the folks in the back:

The biggest problem business owners have is that they don't know what their biggest problem is.

We sure as hell don't, because every problem seems like the big problem—a fire that needs to be put out before it becomes a blazing inferno. I suspect you may feel this way about your business right now. Or you may think you know the exact thing that you need to fix, that thing that, if you could only solve it, would finally make everything work. Shoot, you may have a list neatly tracking *all* the things you need to address to finally achieve the goals you have set. You may even believe that the solution is just to keep grinding it out. (It isn't.) Yet even when you do manage to successfully tackle a problem, or even all those problems, it doesn't seem to move your business forward in a big way.

In the past, I repeatedly fell into the trap of fixing whatever problem was in front of me. Whether I was saving the day, or just trying to get my company to the next level, I rushed to the apparent problems. You know, the obvious stuff and the squeaky wheels. Because—and I know you get this—at any given time there is always a boatload of problems that need your attention. So, trusting my gut instincts, I would just pick the one that felt like the most urgent and focus on that. In this process of addressing the apparent issues, I was disregarding the most impactful one. What resulted was a continuous run of problem solving, and yet my business remained stuck.

Sometimes—rarely, but sometimes—you solve a problem and your business *does* take a leap forward. Phew. The relief. You see positive movement. In that moment, the future looks so bright you gotta wear shades (made of gold). Everything is perfect, until it's not.

Before you know it, your business careens back into the struggle. That's why this outcome is worse—tasting success only to get stuck again is not just frustrating, it's costly and demoralizing. I call this the Survival Trap. Sadly, I have found it to be the most common situation in which entrepreneurs find themselves. They take the necessary (and often panicked) actions to keep the business alive today, and then repeat the pattern tomorrow, and the tomorrow after that, and so on. The goal for each day is simply to survive the day.

The Survival Trap manifests in many different ways. If you've read my previous books, you might be familiar with it. When it comes to our business's (lack of) cash flow, we often throw our few remaining dollars at the immediate problems and opportunities, hoping that profit will magically materialize as a result. When it comes to our time, we burn out ourselves and our people by working even longer hours, constantly putting out fires and chasing arbitrary quarterly targets instead of building sustainable systems. And when it comes to fixing the business, we find ourselves patching up the obvious problems, only to wonder why they keep reoccurring over and over again.

If this cycle seems a little too real and you're wondering if it's even possible to break out of it, take heart. Entrepreneurs are natural problem solvers. You are a natural problem solver. You can't get a business off the ground without being one. So it's not as if your business is being held back because you're up against an unsolvable problem. You can fix whatever it is that's holding you back . . . if only you can figure out what you need to fix, and in what order.

You *can* move your business forward in big strides, and in short order. Your vision for your business *can* become a reality. And it *will*, once you figure out what your biggest problem is right now, and then devote yourself to fixing that next.

You Can't Get out of the Woods on Instinct Alone

Amanda Eller intended to take a brief hike in the Hawaiian woods but ended up lost for seventeen days, clinging to life. Eller's plan was to go on a three-mile hike. At one point, she sat down on a log to meditate. When she finished, she wanted to return to her car, but she was disoriented and unsure which way to go.

"I have a strong sense of internal guidance, whatever you want to call that—a voice, spirit, everybody has a different name for it," she told reporters after the rescue team found her. Except, it turned out, her "internal guide" seemed to be on the fritz that day. And continued to fail her for sixteen more consecutive days. She tried one path, and then another. She even ended up on a path that was not for humans—it was a boar path. Yup. You read that right. Her internal guide sent her on a boar path. You know, those half feral pig, half mini-rhino beasts that try to impale you if you look at them the wrong way. That boar path.

When rescuers found Eller, she was severely injured (not from a boar, which was a small mercy), could barely move, and had given up all hope of being found. She was only a few miles from her car.

So what might have helped Eller find a path out of the woods? She admitted later that she was irresponsible and should have brought her cell phone and some water. She also didn't have a compass in case her cell phone battery died or she couldn't find service to use the map app on her phone. The magic of a compass is that when you have one, there's no need for batteries or phone chargers or GPS, it can work in any weather condition, and it is ready to go twenty-four seven—whenever you need it. If Amanda had had a basic compass, just a simple, fit-in-your-pocket, no-bells-and-whistles compass (and knew how to use it), she would have made it home safe and sound in time for dinner.

I've always been a big believer in working *with* my human nature to accomplish a goal, rather than trying to *change* my wiring to achieve it. Why go the long way around the block? Or take a seventeen-day, life-threatening detour through the woods? That's why I designed the Profit First system to work with our natural tendency to manage our business by our bank accounts. In the past, I would spend all I had, based on how much cash was sitting in my bank that day, even though I knew that I had to set aside some of it for taxes or for a big equipment purchase. I would always try *not* to spend down my bank balance, but it was a game of wills. And I almost always lost that game.

By simply allocating my revenue into profit and other accounts, such as a reserve for taxes, I ensured that when I spent my operating expense account down, I still had enough money for everything else—especially profit.

So what we really need are systems that work *with* our natural tendencies. You can still use your gut to navigate the terrain, but a compass will ensure your instincts are in fact consistently moving you in the right direction. In much the same way, Fix This Next is a simple system that works like a compass for your business. When I use this system, it always points me in the direction I need to go, and I use my instincts to address the immediate terrain. And you will too.

Getting your business bearings begins with what you see as a barrier to your company's path forward, and then, in four simple steps, home in on the direction you need to take (that is, the problem you need to solve).

The Business Hierarchy of Needs

Chances are you've heard the common belief that the actions you need to take to drive growth should be determined by the stage of revenue your business is at. For example, "they" say when you achieve $250,000 in annual revenue, you will likely need a full-time employee. When you get to $1 million, you will probably need to master niche specialization. At $5 million, you'll need to build a cache of cash. When you hit $10 million, systems are everything. I understand this thinking, and although these are occasionally applicable guidelines, they don't hold much water in our times.

On its own, revenue is not a reliable marker for healthy business growth. A business doing $250,000 in annual revenue could be more successful than a business doing $250 million.* In fact, a small business can bring more joy to the owners, have a higher profit percentage, be more efficient, have a greater impact on their industry and community, and create a remarkable legacy that far surpasses a company that has one hundred times the sales.

---

*Sadly, as I was writing this section, a very good friend of mine who was running the $250 million company he founded filed for Chapter 11. They were crushed by an inability to deliver their services as quickly as they needed to to sustain a healthy cash flow.

The old model of business stages tied to revenue is too narrow a perspective for modern businesses. It's also rooted, in part, by ego. Why do we want to build a multimillion-dollar business? Is it because that number will fuel predetermined personal and professional goals? Or is it because we want to be able to *say* we built a multimillion-dollar business? We need to be honest with ourselves and admit that our revenue goals are often arbitrary, and sometimes, just sometimes, based on a need to hear our friends say, "Dang, dawg! That's impressive, yo!" (Or however your weirdo bowling buddies would say it.)

I believe there is a better model to help illuminate the right business strategies, and you may already be familiar with it. In 1943, Abraham Maslow identified what has now become known as Maslow's hierarchy of needs. Originally presented in a journal article titled "A Theory of Human Motivation," Maslow's theory states that there are five categories of human need. From the most basic and essential needs for survival to the highest needs for happiness and fulfillment, they are:

1. *Physiological:* These are the most critical needs for human survival, and include necessities such as air, food, water, shelter, sex, and sleep.
2. *Safety:* At this second stage, humans are focused on a secure and safe environment, health, and financial security.
3. *Belongingness:* Moving up to the third stage, we seek love, friendship, community, family, and intimacy.
4. *Esteem:* In the fourth stage, humans focus on confidence, self-esteem, self-worth, achievement, and respect.

5. *Self-Actualization:* At the fifth stage, the highest level, humans thirst for morality, creativity, and self-expression, and to help others achieve self-actualization. Maslow argued it is at this level that we realize our full potential.

You're a smart cookie, so even if you've never heard of Maslow's hierarchy of needs, you can probably figure out that in order for us to attend to something higher on the list, we first need to make sure that our needs are met in the categories below it. So, for example, before you can focus on meeting your needs for love and belonging, you first need the basics: air to breathe, adequate hydration and nutrition, and a safe place to sleep. It's pretty tough to deal with your self-actualization when you're tired *and* hangry.

Even when we humans *do* have all of our basic needs met in our everyday lives, we sometimes find ourselves back at the bottom of

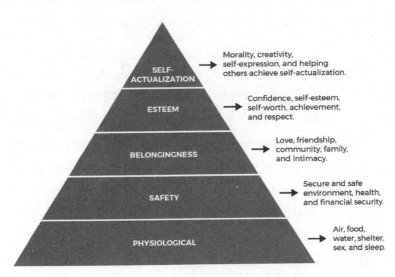

Figure 1. Maslow's Hierarchy of Needs

the pyramid. You could be self-actualizing with the best of them while munching down a double bacon cheeseburger, and none of that matters the second a piece of Angus lodges in your windpipe. Suddenly, you are forced to deal with one of the most basic needs: air. It isn't about intellectual contemplation anymore. Now it is all about, and only about, getting that hunk of meat out of your throat.

What does any of this have to do with running a business? Looking at Maslow's hierarchy of needs, I realized that it has a direct correlation to entrepreneurial progress: what drives your business, what keeps your company trapped, and how you fix the roadblocks along the way to achieve the highest levels of success as you, the entrepreneur, define it. It's all there in Maslow's hierarchy, just with some tweaks and changes to fit the dynamics of business.

Exactly as Maslow argued, we must first meet our base-level needs before we can focus on advanced levels such as love, belonging, and self-actualization. Similarly, a healthy company must first attend to the base needs of sales, profit, and order before the leadership (you) can focus on more advanced pursuits, such as impact and legacy. The key to climbing the hierarchy is simple: fully satisfy your business's *current* level of needs, not by rushing to the apparent daily demands, not by addressing advanced needs before basic needs, and certainly not by trying to fix everything at once. To do this, we will use what I call the Business Hierarchy of Needs (BHN).

The model looks like this, starting with the most essential:

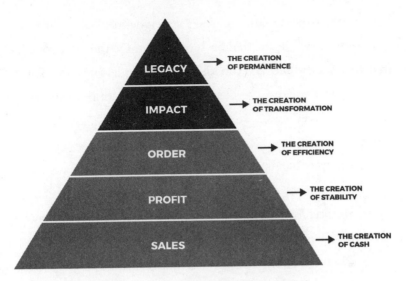

Figure 2. The Business Hierarchy of Needs

Within each level, there are "needs" that must be adequately met before you can focus on a higher level. So just as we humans need to ensure we have food and water before we can start to address our self-esteem, your business must first focus on its basic needs. After three years of research and redos (and banging my head against the wall a few times), I have identified five Core Needs within each of the five levels of the BHN. They are listed below, and we'll get into each one in greater detail in chapters 3 through 8.

Sales

At this foundational level, the business must focus on the creation of cash. Just as humans can't survive without oxygen, food, and water, if you don't have sales, your company will not be able to survive for long. Heck, without sales, you won't have a business at all. Addressing the five needs in the SALES level will ensure that your foundation is working solidly and can support the next level, PROFIT.

Here are the five Core Needs and corresponding questions for the SALES level:

1. *Lifestyle Congruence:* Do you know what the company's sales performance must be to support your personal comfort?
2. *Prospect Attraction:* Do you attract enough quality prospects to support your needed sales?
3. *Client Conversion:* Do you convert enough of the right prospects into clients to support your needed sales?
4. *Delivering on Commitments:* Do you fully deliver on your commitments to your clients?
5. *Collecting on Commitments:* Do your clients fully deliver on their commitments to you?

Profit

At the PROFIT level, the company's focus shifts to the creation of stability. Here, our business's needs line up pretty closely with our human needs for health, financial stability, and a secure and safe environment. Massive revenue doesn't mean much when you have no profit, no cash reserves, and are drowning in debt. When all five needs in the PROFIT level are satisfied, you are positioned to scale your business without financial collapse.

Here are the five Core Needs and corresponding questions for the PROFIT level:

1. *Debt Eradication:* Do you consistently remove debt rather than accumulate it?
2. *Margin Health:* Do you have healthy profit margins within each of your offerings and do you continually seek ways to improve them?
3. *Transaction Frequency:* Do your clients repeatedly buy from you over alternatives?
4. *Profitable Leverage:* When debt is used, is it used to generate predictable, increased profitability?
5. *Cash Reserves:* Does the business have enough cash reserves to cover all expenses for three months or longer?

Order

At this level, the focus is on the creation of efficiency, and the needs are related to ensuring that everything runs like clockwork. With all of its organizational efficiency needs met, your business can run—and yes, even grow—no matter who is on your team. It can even grow without *you*, the business owner.

Here are the five Core Needs and corresponding questions for the ORDER level:

1. *Minimized Wasted Effort:* Do you have an ongoing and working model to reduce bottlenecks, slowdowns, and inefficiencies?
2. *Role Alignment:* Are people's roles and responsibilities matched to their talents?
3. *Outcome Delegation:* Are the people closest to the problem empowered to resolve it?

4. *Linchpin Redundancy:* Is your business designed to operate unabated when key employees are not available?

5. *Mastery Reputation:* Are you known for being the best in your industry at what you do?

Impact

The focus now is on the creation of transformation. Many businesses never properly address the needs at this level, because they either don't know this level exists, or misunderstand what it's all about. When we think of impact, we think of how our business impacts the world. However, the needs that must be addressed at this level are related to client transformation, and how your company aligns with your staff, vendors, and your community, not to the wider world.

Here are the five Core Needs and corresponding questions for the IMPACT level:

1. *Transformation Orientation:* Does your business benefit clients through a transformation, beyond the transaction?

2. *Mission Motivation:* Are all employees (including leadership) motivated more by delivering on the mission than by their individual roles?

3. *Dream Alignment:* Are people's individual dreams aligned with the path of the business's grand vision?

4. *Feedback Integrity:* Are your people, clients, and community empowered to give both critical and complimentary feedback?

5. *Complementary Network:* Does your business seek to collaborate with vendors (including competitors) who serve the same customer base in order to improve the customer experience?

▼
▼
▼
▼
▼

Legacy

At this highest level, the focus is on the creation of permanence. Ensuring that your business and the impact it delivers will live on after you move on requires that specific needs are met. If you want your business to continue to thrive for generations to come, you'll have to consider the big questions, such as what your long-term vision for your company is, and how your business will adapt to changes in your industry, in consumer demand, and in the world.

Here are the five Core Needs and corresponding questions for the LEGACY level:

1. *Community Continuance:* Do your clients fervently defend, support, and help the business?
2. *Intentional Leadership Turn:* Is there a plan for leadership to transition and stay fresh?
3. *Heart-based Promoters:* Is the organization promoted by individuals inside and outside the organization, without need of direction?
4. *Quarterly Dynamics:* Does your business have a clear vision for its future and dynamically adjust quarterly to make that vision become true?

5. *Ongoing Adaptation:* Is the business designed to constantly adapt and improve, including finding ways to better and best itself?

To be clear, the BHN levels do *not* represent stages in business growth. They are levels of needs. Your business will not climb the hierarchy in a linear fashion, but move up and down levels as it progresses. Like building and renovating structures, you don't just go up. You go back down to the foundation, shore it up, so you can build higher. So, for example, while you may be dealing with a need in the SALES level, that does not mean your company is still in the SALES stage. You are simply strengthening the foundation.

I'm pretty sure I know what you're thinking: *This list may work for your business, but my business is different.* Your business may very well have additional needs. While this list is not comprehensive, each of the five Core Needs at each of the five levels are required for every business to be healthy and thriving. If you have a need that is *not* listed on the BHN, jot it down and save it for later. I ask that you trust the process and, for this first go-round, focus on the five essentials of each level on the BHN.

Most business owners try to master all things at once. It was my modus operandi for years. I intended to *simultaneously* have impact, make lots of money, work whenever I wanted to, create a legacy, and have clients flocking to my company. The thing is, prioritizing everything at the same time means that *nothing* is a priority. Just like Maslow's hierarchy, all these elements are in play at all times. However, you can only concentrate your energy on solving one

THE 5 CORE NEEDS FOR SALES
☐ Lifestyle Congruence
☐ Prospect Attraction
☐ Client Conversion
☐ Delivering on Commitments
☐ Collecting on Commitments

THE 5 CORE NEEDS FOR ORDER
☐ Minimized Wasted Effort
☐ Role Alignment
☐ Outcome Delegation
☐ Linchpin Redundancy
☐ Mastery Reputation

THE 5 CORE NEEDS FOR LEGACY
☐ Community Continuance
☐ Intentional Leadership Turn
☐ Heart-based Promoters
☐ Quarterly Dynamics
☐ Ongoing Adaptation

THE 5 CORE NEEDS FOR PROFIT
☐ Debt Eradication
☐ Margin Health
☐ Transaction Frequency
☐ Profitable Leverage
☐ Cash Reserves

THE 5 CORE NEEDS FOR IMPACT
☐ Transformation Orientation
☐ Mission Motivation
☐ Dream Alignment
☐ Feedback Integrity
☐ Complementary Network

Figure 3. The BHN with the Five Core Needs of Each Level

issue within one level at a time. The golden rule is always to satisfy the most essential need (the one closest to the base), before addressing a need above it.

Let's say you have a consistent stream of sales, and it supports the goals you have clearly outlined. If that is true, then your business has achieved the equivalent of breathing in air. The next level is PROFIT, which translates to safety and security. If someone is trying to rob you by holding a knife to your chest, you don't worry about air (SALES); you worry about getting out of danger. But if suddenly you and the guy with the knife are trapped in a room with no oxygen (SALES), you would *both* be focused on the more urgent need—finding the air you need to breathe.

You are instinctually wired to find the air you need to breathe, the water and food you need to survive, and to avoid danger. But for entrepreneurs, the solution to our business problems are in fact *not* instinctual. The business is its own entity, so you don't have biological triggers telling you that your business is thirsty, or starving, or just needs some cuddle time. We *think* we are connected to our business in that way. (We're not.) So we "trust our gut" and make what feels like appropriate decisions to grow.

If you find yourself walking down a dark alley and something just doesn't feel right, that is your instinct indicating something is wrong. I suggest you turn around fast and find another way to get where you are going, because if you don't, you might just end up in the hospital. Your senses—seeing, hearing, smelling—are all directly wired into your brain, providing immediate and helpful insights. While we are wired into our bodies, we are *not* wired into our business, and that poses a problem. Instincts save lives. Businesses? Not so much.

The thing is, we all *believe* we have good business instincts—that we can trust our gut to help us make the right decisions. And yet very often we end up like Amanda Eller, walking down a boar path in search of our way out. We are fixing the *wrong thing* at the *wrong time*. The most common, gut instinct solution that I see employed by entrepreneurs is this: sell more. For example, a business may have a relatively consistent degree of sales, yet the business is not profitable. Rather than try to resolve the PROFIT level, we almost inexplicably revert to trying to sell more, believing that more SALES (the most basic level) will fix the PROFIT level. For Maslow's hierarchy this is akin to being caught up in a brawl (the Safety Level) and gasping for air to protect ourselves (the Physiological Level). It makes no sense. Even though, biologically speaking, we would have a fight-or-flight response; since we aren't wired into our business instinctually we gasp for air while we get punched in the face, repeatedly. Other times, a business is unable to deliver on time and as promised consistently, which is an ORDER-level problem. Yet the owner's instinct is to sell more, amp up revenue, and expect that will somehow fix the business operations. It doesn't, and it won't.

These trust-your-gut and shoot-from-the-hip methods of growing a business very often impede success. Some businesses are successful not because of, but in spite of, the entrepreneur at the helm. Without a specific, repeatable strategy to growth, their success is more like a lottery win than an architected plan.

What we need is a compass. Something that we can use to check our gut instincts, to make sure we are in fact moving true north. That is what the BHN will do for you.

What We Believe May Not Be True

Recently, I became fascinated with the story of the Winchester Mystery House, a sprawling, 160-plus-room Queen Anne Victorian mansion in San Jose, California. Once I read about this house, I immediately booked a flight to San Jose, toured the bizarre structure, and discovered an uncanny parallel to the typical entrepreneur's journey.

When Sarah Winchester's husband died of tuberculosis in 1881, he left her a fortune worth more than $500 million in today's dollars. William Winchester was a gun magnate, and heir to the Winchester Repeating Arms Company. Legend has it that Sarah believed she was haunted by the ghosts of people who were killed using Winchester rifles, and that she needed to build more and more rooms onto her home to satisfy (and hide from) the evil spirits chasing her.

Sarah moved to California, bought a two-story, eight-room farmhouse, and proceeded to build additions. Relentlessly.

Thirty-eight years later, she was still building.

With no rhyme or reason, and no architect to help her plan, Sarah set out to add new room after new room. According to Miranda of the *Spooky Little Halloween* blog, "Sarah would build whatever she felt like, often abandoning ideas and building around errors her workers made. She met with her foreman every morning to go over her hand-sketched plans for the day's work." Sarah would start every day's work by tackling the most apparent issue of the day.

I don't know about you, but I think Sarah needed an architected plan (and maybe a skosh of therapy). She believed in her instinct alone, and then every day she tried to figure out how to appease or get away from the problems (ghosts) she saw.

Eventually, what was once a farmhouse became a seven-story mansion with more than 160 rooms—rooms she built and then never set foot in again. Doors and windows opened up to walls, many fireplaces had no chimneys, and some staircases led to nowhere.

When the San Francisco earthquake hit in 1906, all of the top three stories were destroyed, and part of the fourth. The damaged areas were not restored, but instead were picked for supplies to build elsewhere. Today, what's left of the Winchester Mystery Mansion covers roughly 24,000 square feet and has more than 10,000 windows, and 6 kitchens. It's one of the strangest houses I've ever seen, and it is a weirdo's paradise. (Between you and me, I think I saw one of your bowling buddies there.) Get to Googling and see for yourself. When you do, think about your business. Think about all the choices you made based on instinct, or in response to a problem (an evil spirit), or to counterpunch a competitor (an evil-er spirit), or just because it is what an "expert" said you needed. Think about all of the "rooms" you built and maybe even abandoned trying to jump on opportunities, or solve problems, or just because you didn't know what else to do.

Upon Sarah Winchester's passing, construction immediately stopped. Her house went on the market, yet the massive mansion was unsellable. No one wanted the extraordinary, complex, and confusing house, nor did anyone have enough funds or expertise to fix it. Ultimately, an investor group purchased the house for pennies on the dollar and made it into an exhibit for seekers of the odd and extreme. A massive structure, under continuous construction for nearly forty years, it was ultimately worthless (except as a perfect illustration of what I am about to tell you).

When you trust your gut alone instead of analyzing your business, you could end up with useless fireplaces and stairs to nowhere. Or lost in a Hawaiian forest. So as tuned in and savvy as I know you are, I'm asking you to forgo your reliance on instinct alone . . . at least for as long as it takes you to read this book and implement the action steps. Okay? Can we (virtually) shake on that? In other words, humor me.

The BHN may not be as mystical as the séance Harry Houdini held in the Winchester house one evening (true story), but give it a try. It just may save your company, and your sanity.

Here's a simple but powerful challenge: I have found that the most effective way to improve your business is to commit to another person your intentions to improve. So, here I am, your new account-ability partner. Email me at Mike@MikeMichalowicz.com with the subject line "I'm doing FTN!" so I can quickly find it. In your email tell me why you're committed to the FTN process and what it will mean to you as you realize the dream you have for your business. With your commitment documented, your likelihood of seeing it through will skyrocket. Plus, it will be awesome for us to connect. Let's do this!

As I mentioned earlier, I have prepared free powerful resources and tools for you that supplement this book. Go to FixThisNext .com right now to get them. When you visit the site be sure to take the free evaluation. It will pinpoint what you need to fix next in your business. And you can be resolving it minutes from now.

A QUICK NOTE ABOUT PROFIT FIRST

Before we get rolling fully into *Fix This Next*, I need to address a thought you might be having about another book I wrote: *Profit First*. When talking about FTN, people ask me, "Mike, didn't you say we should take our profit first? If profit always comes first, how could you suggest addressing other things first in *Fix This Next*? You sound like a big, fat, smelly hypocrite."

The smelly part you can blame on my bad genetics.

The rest simply needs clarification.

When I wrote *Profit First*, I challenged the traditional formula of profitability: sales − expenses = profit. Simply put, traditional thinking teaches us that profit comes last. That profit is the bottom line. And *that* is the problem with the old formula. It is human nature that when something comes last, it gets delayed at best and ignored most often.

Profit First means that profit comes *before* expenses. Sales − profit = expenses. Take your profit *first*, put it into an account, and hide it away from your business, before you spend a single dime. Profit First means you allocate your profit first and then you are forced to reverse engineer your way to achieving the profit you already took. It is the pay-yourself-first principle applied to business. Profit First does *not* mean that profit is the only thing you focus on and that you can ignore everything else.

To improve your business, identify the most important thing your business needs at this moment and then fix it. At times it will be at the level of SALES, or ORDER. At other times it will be at the level of PROFIT, or IMPACT, or LEGACY. I suggest that once you implement Profit First, you continue to use it—as in forever. And once your profit is shored up, your next—as in, top, or first—priority will be the next thing your Fix This Next compass points to.

If you haven't implemented Profit First yet, I suggest that you put the idea on pause until you finish this book. Because, as strange as it may sound hearing this from me, your profit may not come first (or next). You may have another Vital Need you must address before profit. I am sure Profit First will serve you, but until you finish this process, we can't say in absolute terms *when* it will *best* serve you.

Hope that clears it up. Profit First is the formula of taking profit first. It is *not* about prioritizing profit at all times and above everything else. We good? Good.

Chapter 2

FIND IT AND FIX IT

"YEAH, BUT . . ."

I'm always amazed by how many of us business owners have a serious case of the "yeah, but's." We believe our companies are so unique that simple solutions and strategies could not possibly help us with whatever problem we think we have. "Yeah, but my business is different," we shout from the rooftops. I get it. I thought that was true for my businesses too. Maybe you feel your business is special too. But the thing is, it's not even a wee bit true.

Just as our human DNA is 99.9 percent identical, the DNA for all businesses is nearly identical. I don't care if you run a farm or a pharmacy. I don't care if you invest, divest, suggest, or profess for a living. Your business is 99.9 percent identical to all others—just as they are nearly identical to yours. The remaining 0.1 percent of our DNA is the skin of our corporate bodies. Our businesses may look different on the outside. You may have different equipment and people with different skill sets. Your office may be virtual or physical or nonexistent. That's just the skin of the business. What is under your corporate skin is nearly equivalent to all other businesses.

Before Ken Mulvey started his business, Supply Patriot, he was a bodyguard to the rich and famous. In one of our conversations, he shared some details of the protection services he provided for a key executive of a major publisher. As he recounted the story, I was thinking, "So the publisher gets a bodyguard, but the measly author guy gets squat? Nice. Real nice."

As part of his guard work, Ken attended board meetings. You know, because you never know when a thug is going to break into a conference room to steal old crusty doughnuts and stale coffee from old crusty guys with stale breath. Ken's job was to be on the watch, and since there was nothing to watch out for (refer to my prior point) he would listen. Closely.

"Mike, there were some of the biggest CEOs in the country serving on that board," Ken told me. "And they all had the identical problems that my friends' small businesses had, only with five or six more zeros at the end of every number. They had the same cash-flow problems, the same hiring problems, the same profitability problems. The same confusion over what to do next."

Ken's story reminded me of a conversation I had with a friend who owns a $22 million company. We were in a room with one hundred business owners at the Gathering of Titans annual meeting in Dedham, Massachusetts.

I've known my friend Stu for almost twenty years. We grew up together as entrepreneurs, and I've seen his company grow. A lot.

Although it fits the U.S. government's definition of a "small business" (less than $25 million in sales), Stu's company is *the* leader in their space. In fact, I suspect you would recognize its name. You would probably recognize Stu's real name too, which is why I am not using either in this book.

During a break, I asked Stu a simple question that, when you have a true friendship, can open the door to deep conversations and confessions.

"How it's going, Stu?"

"Great," he said with a half smile.

I know that smile. I've seen it on the faces of thousands of entrepreneurs, and I've seen it on my own face when I look in the mirror.

"Oh, no. What's wrong, brother?" I asked.

He sighed, did the look-over-both-shoulders move, and then replied in a hushed tone, "I only have four weeks of cash left in my business, Mike. I have no prospects. At least, not enough prospects to keep us alive."

This is not an unusual scenario for most small-business owners, but how could this happen to a $22 million industry leader? It had to be a fluke, right? Nope. Some of the most successful entrepreneurs in the world were in this room, and yet you might be surprised to discover that, at any given time, 10 to 20 percent of them are in deep shit.

Whether your business is big, small, or somewhere in between, the needs are exactly the same. Size doesn't matter, after all. Nor does revenue or number of employees or the number of years you have operated your (possibly crusty and stale) business.

I totally get that your business has unique qualities. Just like mine. Just like all businesses. All people have unique qualities too, yet we all share a common biology. These unique qualities are necessary and critical, because we need differentiators to attract our ideal customers. When we're talking marketing and branding, different is better. But we're not talking about that in this book. What we are talking about today is the biology of your business.

Just as all humans need to follow the same basic parameters to grow and maintain health, the methods to achieving growth and sustaining health are nearly identical for almost every business. Ours may look different from the outside. Ours may do different things. But never forget this: the essential makeup of almost all businesses is nearly identical. One guy may run a pizza shop and another gal might have a flight-instruction business. But the way they sustain themselves and grow, and the crucial needs they need to meet, are the same.

In this chapter, you'll learn a simple process to navigate the Business Hierarchy of Needs (BHN) so you can find what to fix next, and a simple method to find a solution so you can fix it and move on.

Find It

Let's pretend we're playing a game of tug-of-war, except instead of a rope we pull on opposite ends of a metal chain, and instead of trying to pull each other over a line, our aim is to find where the chain breaks. You take one end and, standing a few feet away, I have the other. Between us are twenty-five or so links of the chain. On the count of three, we both start pulling to see where it breaks.

No matter how we pull on the chain, neither of us has any control over where it will break.

The chain will always break at the weakest link. In other words, any chain is only as strong as its weakest link. No matter what you try, you can't manipulate the process to make a different part of it break. It has a natural weak spot. If you want to strengthen the entirety of the chain you must address its weakest link, which, in the context of your business, I call the Vital Need. At any moment, of all the Core Needs that exist within your business there is a single Vital Need that represents the current weakest link. You can't manipulate the "game" to make it something different. Your job is to find it and then fix it next, before you move on to what emerges as the new Vital Need.

Within any business process, be it the finer details of how you build your product, or the broader sequence your prospects go through to become your clients, there are chains of events. At all levels of a business's development, from struggling startup to industry titan, everything goes through a chain of events. Within this chain there will always only ever be one link that is the weakest. The goal of this book is to help you find that weakest link and strengthen it, because when you strengthen the weakest link the entire chain is strengthened.

Eliyahu Goldratt introduced the Theory of Constraints in his must-read book, *The Goal*. According to the Theory of Constraints, a business process can only operate as fast as its slowest part. Therefore, if you want to improve the overall output of your business process, you seek out the highest priority constraint, open it up, and the entire business will now perform at the speed of the next biggest constraint.

As I shared in chapter 1, and as you undoubtedly know all too well, the common approach to growing a business is to grow everything at once. We need more sales! We need to make more money! We need to hire employees who act like owners! We need to stand out from our competition! We need to change the world! We need better marketing, better sales, better products, better services, better efficiency, better everything, and we better get a better attitude from everyone, right now. Damn it!! While it may be true that your business needs all of the above, if you try to make everything better at the same time, you will dilute your energy, time, and focus, and find yourself unable to meet even one of those needs satisfactorily.

Once you have identified the most Vital Need you face, you'll then apply the fix with all the available resources you've got.

Using the BHN as your checklist, here are the steps to figuring out which Core Need is your Vital Need and the one you must fix next:

STEP 1—*Identify:* Within each level, check off the Core Needs that your company is adequately meeting to support the level above it. If you aren't adequately meeting a need or don't know, leave it unchecked.

STEP 2—*Pinpoint:* Evaluate the lowest level that has unchecked Core Needs. So if you have unchecked needs in PROFIT, IMPACT, and LEGACY, work at the lowest level of the three: PROFIT. Of the needs you left unchecked at that level, which one is most crucial at this moment? Circle this as your Vital Need.

STEP 3—Fulfill: Generate measurable solutions for the circled Vital Need. Implement your solutions until the Vital Need is adequately addressed.

STEP 4—Repeat: With the Vital Need fixed, find the next Vital Need by repeating the three steps above. Use this process for the life of your business to navigate through challenges, maximize opportunities, and continually uplevel your business.

Following this process doesn't mean you can ignore the rest of your business—you need to keep those plates spinning. It goes without question that you need to service many parts of your business at all times. You can't suddenly tell your customers, "Hey! We're just going to ignore you for a few months, while we take care of some internal stuff. Talk to you soon. Oh, and please keep sending us your money in the meantime, my beeyotches."

You can't grind the business to a halt while you work only on the next Vital Need. Using Fix This Next, we identify the biggest problem that, when fixed, will unleash the most forward momentum for the business. Instead of doing everything all the time, we will continue to maintain the necessary effort and allocate remaining resources to fully serve the next Vital Need.

Addressing your business's most Vital Need may require you to make tough decisions. You may need to make sacrifices to fix the problem. For example, if you determine that your Vital Need requires you to fix a collections problem, the only fix may be to fire the clients who chronically pay late. Facing the loss of short-term revenue, however temporary, may stop you in your tracks. The temptation may be to take on less-than ideal clients or work you are not well suited to do, or don't like doing, so that you can "make up" the temporary short-term loss. Welcome back to the Survival Trap, buddy. The only way out is to hold the line—do what you need to do to make sure that you build your business in a healthy manner, not based on your desperation.

I feel there are a couple of sexy things about the BHN: First, the whole "two birds, one stone" thing. When you identify a Vital Need at a lower level, you may find that resolving that need resolves a higher-level need.

Second, perhaps the coolest aspect of the BHN: as you fix the Vital Need, it leverages all the work you already put into your business. In fact, sometimes levels can be resolved and cleared with little effort, maybe even in minutes. You do not need to reinvent the wheel here. You just need to bring a Vital Need to conclusion, something you may already have been doing without acute awareness.

Using the BHN and these four steps will help you break through almost any plateau, quickly resolve setbacks, and grow your business in a sustainable way. Whatever goals you set for your business will be much, much easier to reach and much, much more likely to sustain.

As you continue to repeat the four-step Fix This Next analysis, your business foundation becomes stronger and stronger, ensuring that your vision for your business becomes reality.

The FTN Analysis in Practice

When I first met Tersh Blissett, I instantly knew he was one of "my peeps." How did I know? Because he was wearing a vest.

I wear a vest every time I deliver a keynote. It's my thang. My team likes to make fun of me for my "costume." Kelsey Ayres, who I am beyond blessed to have as a colleague, occasionally wears a T-shirt to work that reads "Live Your VEST Life" next to a picture of me in one of my uncoolest denim vests. Cute.

Occasionally, I host a free conference at my offices in New Jersey to share and test out my newest concepts. (If you want to attend one of these free presentations, simply sign up to "get the tools" on my website at MikeMichalowicz.com and keep an eye out for one of my out-of-the-blue announcements inviting you to my next free thing.) Tersh attended my first-ever live presentation on Fix This Next. He sat near the front, and because he was wearing a pressed shirt, narrow tie, and a killer vest, I assumed he had a financial business, or that maybe he was, you know, a badass, awesome, amazing, supercool business author guy. I mean, who else can pull off a vest so well? I soon learned that I was dead wrong: Tersh owns IceBound HVAC & Refrigeration in Savannah, Georgia. He doesn't just wear a vest, he's an air-conditioning guru. Which makes him ridiculously cool. (Get it?)

Talking with him for just a few minutes, I knew we had more in common than our fashion sense; I had met a soul mate. Tersh is kind, driven, and smart as a whip. He is an entrepreneur through and through and is doing everything he can to grow a healthy business.

After the conference concluded, Tersh was the first to give me feedback on which aspects of Fix This Next were helpful and which weren't. As I further enhanced and simplified the system, I was in constant touch with Tersh for his feedback. When I finally finished the system as you see it in this book, Tersh was my first call. I gave him the lowdown and asked him to diagnose his business. He sat down with his wife, Julie, who is a partner in the business and called me back later that day.

"Mike," he said, "Julie and I spent less than fifteen minutes with the Fix This Next system and achieved a degree of clarity we never had before. Fifteen minutes and our eyes were wide open. And the funny thing is, ten of those minutes were spent brainstorming solutions for the business's Vital Need. It took only five minutes for us to figure out exactly what we needed to do next."

Prior to learning about the BHN, Tersh was trying to do "everything" to move the business forward. In 2018, IceBound achieved a respectable $750,000 in revenue and was on track to reach $1 million in 2019. Following the Profit First system, his company had reached 12 percent cash profit (in addition to a solid weekly paycheck for Tersh and the business paying *all* of his personal taxes). The business had been running, for the most part, without Tersh's active input.

Tersh's instinct told him to focus on the IMPACT level of his business. He was working on a structure that would be more and more charitable. He believed that donating time and money was the way to serve his community, and this would, in turn, bring in more business.

Tersh then did the Fix This Next analysis. He moved through the checklist level by level, starting at the foundational level of SALES, moving up to PROFIT and so on until he got to LEGACY, checking off the Core Needs his business adequately addressed at each level, and leaving the others unchecked. Within the SALES

THE 5 CORE NEEDS FOR SALES

THE 5 CORE NEEDS FOR PROFIT

THE 5 CORE NEEDS FOR ORDER

THE 5 CORE NEEDS FOR IMPACT

THE 5 CORE NEEDS FOR LEGACY

THE 5 CORE NEEDS FOR SALES
- ☑ Lifestyle Congruence
- ☐ Prospect Attraction
- ☑ Client Conversion
- ☑ Delivering on Commitments
- ☐ Collecting on Commitments

THE 5 CORE NEEDS FOR ORDER
- ☑ Minimized Wasted Effort
- ☐ Role Alignment
- ☑ Outcome Delegation
- ☐ Linchpin Redundancy
- ☐ Mastery Reputation

THE 5 CORE NEEDS FOR LEGACY
- ☑ Community Continuance
- ☐ Intentional Leadership Turn
- ☐ Heart-based Promoters
- ☑ Quarterly Dynamics
- ☐ Ongoing Adaptation

THE 5 CORE NEEDS FOR PROFIT
- ☑ Debt Eradication
- ☐ Margin Health
- ☑ Transaction Frequency
- ☑ Profitable Leverage
- ☐ Cash Reserves

THE 5 CORE NEEDS FOR IMPACT
- ☑ Transformation Orientation
- ☐ Mission Motivation
- ☑ Dream Alignment
- ☐ Feedback Integrity
- ☐ Complementary Network

Figure 4. The BHN with satisfied Core Needs checked

level, Tersh left Prospect Attraction and Collecting on Commitments unchecked. At the PROFIT level, Margin Health, Profitable Leverage, and Cash Reserves were left unchecked. In ORDER, IMPACT, and LEGACY, other items remained unchecked.

Then he and Julie looked at the most foundational level with unchecked needs. In the SALES level, they examined Prospect Attraction and Collecting on Commitments. They were waiting on nearly fifty thousand dollars of accounts receivable, which for a company doing $1 million in revenue is a lot. While about 5 percent of their revenue was waiting for collections, Tersh noticed that his poorly paying clients represented just a couple of big jobs. So even if he resolved the collections issue, the clients he had were not suitable. In fact, he noticed that his big corporate clients ignored IceBound's COD requirement and followed a net 90 payment cycle, and some even reached out *after* ninety days to point to a "problem" with the invoice or some other excuse that would inevitably stretch the payment another ninety days to six months. These corporate clients were crushing cash flow. It was also clear that they had an attraction issue. Not in terms of quantity—they got a ton of inquiries from corporations. The problem with Prospect Attraction was the quality of customer they attracted.

The Vital Need for IceBound was Prospect Attraction. Tersh realized he had been instinctually working at the wrong level. He was focusing on IMPACT instead of SALES. Tersh's business instincts had him walking down the boar path, just like Amanda Eller's "internal guide" did for her.

So, with his BHN compass, Tersh immediately decided to stop IceBound's charitable efforts. This might sound cold and callous. But it is not. The only way you can give effectively is if you have a strong, healthy foundation of getting. Tersh had to strengthen his business first so that he could give in a sustainable way next.

It took them only five minutes flat to find their Vital Need. Then they focused on finding solutions to improve their Prospect Attraction. They considered vehicle wraps, yard signs, search engine optimization, proximity letters, and other marketing ideas to attract their ideal client. That's when the obvious hit them: Before they could market to their ideal client, they first needed to define what they considered to be the ideal client. Any marketing effort would be a hundred times better if it could target exactly the right customer.

Fifteen minutes and Tersh and Julie had aligned their focus on the next thing that would strengthen their business in a big way: an avatar of the ideal customer. At first, coming up with their avatar proved difficult. Tersh and Julie discovered that IceBound's customer demographics seemed to be all over the place. They had a pretty even mix of male and female customers. Some were young professionals; others were retiring executives.

To understand how Tersh and Julie settled on their avatar, you need to get a quick primer on IceBound's technology. Have you ever found yourself sweating under the blankets and then shivering as soon as you throw them off? Turns out, this is not a temperature problem; this is a temperature-plus-humidity problem. According to Tersh, the fix is having the right size equipment to manage both. IceBound's technology monitors the relative humidity, temperature, and dew point so homeowners can have maximum comfort.

Considering the information more deeply, Tersh and Julie realized that what their best customers had in common was that they all placed a high value on their overall comfort. Their ideal clients were professionals in their late forties to early sixties who were empty nesters and who wanted to replace their air-conditioning so that they could avoid that nightly sweat/shiver dance and achieve the perfect temperature. They wanted quality over everything else.

Once they figured out whom to sell to, Tersh and Julie could concentrate their marketing on that avatar, change the sales scripts, and likely allow them to be more specific in the offering. And it might, just might, skyrocket their revenue and profitability within, let's say, thirty days. More on that in a bit.

Tersh and Julie were able to get laser focused on what their company needed. You will achieve that for your business too, and you might even do it in fifteen minutes or less.

Never forget this (as in, highlight this and tattoo it on your forearm): among all the apparent issues your business has, one *and only one* of them will be the most effective one at any specific moment. We can't rely on our instincts to just magically pick it out every time. We humans are fraught with bias and emotion, and our humanness can get in the way of our finding the best solutions. The BHN will become your handy-dandy compass from this day forward, bringing an easy, thoughtful, and methodical process to all considerations in growing your business.

How to Determine If You Got It Right

The question most entrepreneurs ask me when they go through the FTN analysis is: how do I know I've fixed the problem? You want to get it right, but how do you know if you *did* get it right? The answer is: you don't know instinctually. So the only way to be sure that your solution worked is to measure it. (Highlight and tat that one too.)

I learned this lesson the hard way as a young man in college, when I was entrusted by a group of peers to manage one of the most important functions for all humankind: the Wednesday night fraternity party. After successfully navigating the final hell night and being ordained a brother, it fell on me to pull off the next event. (As a shocker to no one—including you—I was also given the coveted Delta Sigma Pi Wise Ass of the Year Award. Which, for punitive reasons, mandates you manage the next party.)

Wednesdays were the kickoff day for the party week at Virginia Tech (Go Hokies!). Wednesday parties built momentum for the Thursday and Friday parties, which would get people revved up for the Saturday all-nighter parties and the Sunday block parties. The weekend parties would then roll into the Monday bar scene, which often bled into the Tuesday house parties, which would get people ready for the new party week . . . starting on Wednesday. It's a miracle any of us graduated from college.

This was the first party I was responsible for, and I was clueless. I had no idea great parties, even frat parties, were planned in advance. Even if I *did* know that great parties were planned out, I wouldn't have known where to start, or how to determine if my efforts worked. For the Delta Sig Wednesday night party, my goal was simple: have an epic party, dude. I didn't really think about how I would know if it was epic, beyond people telling me how epic it was. I had already failed the "be specific and concise" acid test.

I took the frat "investment fund" (which is what we called it) and went to the hardware store. I bought one big rubber garbage can, one sweeping broom, and one pool skimmer. I then went to the grocery store and bought ten pounds of grape Kool-Aid mix. Then I went to the liquor store and bought their entire grain alcohol supply. If I tried to make the same purchases today, it would look like a scene out of *Breaking Bad*. Oh, and I also bought one can of Coca-Cola to be ironic.

Back at the Delta Sig house, I got to work. Meaning, I made the pledges snake the garden hose in through the basement window and mix the Kool-Aid, hose water, and grain alcohol in the garbage can. If you were smart and spent your youth doing productive things rather than attending frat parties, you might be wondering, Why did you need the broom and the water skimmer, Mike? You use the broom to stir the mixture, and you use the pool skimmer to sweep up the contaminants, Pledge.

I have now shared my entire planning and prep for the party. You may notice, I fell way short on step two. I didn't really have a plan for my "epic party" outcome, I just did what my gut told me to do, get grain booze and mix it up. I planned for nothing else. No music. No food. No alternative drinks, except for the one ironic can of Coca-Cola. Best of all, no invites sent to anyone, including the brothers! I mean, I did mention it at the house meeting that afternoon. I recall my announcement being something like, "My bros, epic party tonight at the house!"

A few people showed, some got schwasted, but the party stunk. In the folklore of Delta Sigma Pi's Virginia Tech chapter, this went down as the second-worst party ever. The worst one was hosted the following week by brother Greg Eckler, whose fraternity nickname is Elk-Terd, but I am strictly prohibited from sharing his nickname, so I won't.

I wish I knew then what I know now about how to measure outcomes:

1. First, know what outcome you want to have. Then determine the best ways to achieve the outcome and pursue the easiest, most impactful solution(s).

2. Next, determine how you will know if you have achieved the outcome. This is the measurement that must both show that you achieved it and indicate the progress you are making toward your desired outcome.

3. Then, set an evaluation frequency to monitor your progress toward your outcome. Don't measure so often that you won't have significant data to review, and don't measure so infrequently that you miss opportunities to improve.

4. If according to your measurements you are not making progress, adjust your approach. If you are making progress, keep doing it.

Now that I am out of my frat-bro stage and in my author-guy stage, I have figured out a few things. First of all, I was a moron. Second, I was a complete moron. Beyond that, I've realized a few more things: clarity and specificity about outcomes is key. Instead of having an epic party as my plan, a more specific, measurable outcome would have been better, such as, "I want at least 80 percent of the brothers saying this was the best party of the year." (While 100 percent would be amazing, it would have been unrealistic. Elk-Terd always found a way to undermine me.)

Then I would have asked the brothers, "My dudes, thinking about the, like, *totally epic* parties you've been to, what made them, like, *totally epic*?" I suspect they would have wanted my grain-punch concoction, but they also would have wanted other low-key choices, like kegs of beer, soda, and water. They would have wanted great music and some junk food. And, the number one best idea would have been to tell the brothers in advance and, idea of all ideas, actually invite guests. If I had set a desired outcome and then put a measurement or two in place, I could have figured out how my supplies were working out, and if the RSVPs were piling up to true epic proportions. But I didn't do any of that. And now I am legend (along with Brother Elk-Terd) . . . for sucking at party planning.

Sadly, most entrepreneurs try to do epic things in their business, too, and the outcomes fall flat. They sit there with not much to show for their efforts but a garbage can reeking of the sweet stench of grain-spiked grape Kool-Aid. The problem is, we don't know what to do next, and we don't have specific target outcomes for the strategies we do employ, nor do we have measurements in place to determine if we achieved them.

Some entrepreneurs do have the clarity, using the BHN, and as a result grow their business faster and more healthily than ever before. Tersh and Julie knew that the next basic need their business had to resolve was Prospect Attraction, and to do that, they created an ideal client avatar by looking at the qualities of their best customers, those customers who paid a premium for their HVAC services and valued the work they did. Then they would start the cloning process, which, if you want details, is explained in *The Pumpkin Plan*.* But remember your new Fix This Next discipline: first pinpoint what you need to fix before exploring books or resources to fix it. Okay? Okay!

---

*Get the book and free resources at PumpkinPlan.com.

With this realization, Tersh and Julie put a measurable plan in place. Instead of their traditional marketing house by house, Ice-Bound saw the opportunity in the C-suite. Tersh knows how many prospects he needs each week for growth, so coming up with the specific outcome was easy. He told me, "If I can get three new executive prospects a week, that will position me for serious growth with my best customers." See how simple that is? All IceBound has to do is track their number of qualified prospects each week. If they get at least three from the C-suite, they're golden. If they fall short, they need to adjust their marketing.

Tersh targeted the ideal avatar on social media so only homeowners who were professionals with older children saw the ads. Then he went for the mother of influencers: real estate agents. When you buy a house, often you address the HVAC systems. Real estate agents know the demographics, so Tersh set up a referral system, thanking agents for introductions to his avatar with a referral fee and impossible-to-get tickets to events. Like, true story, tickets to see my pals the Savannah Bananas. I love it when something comes full circle.[*]

He also declined marginal opportunities, saying no to people who were not the ideal avatar. He said no to price shoppers and sent them to the competitors. As Tersh said, "Our avatar wants superior service over a cheap price, and if someone asks for a cheap price, we know they are not our avatar and we decline the opportunity immediately."

---

[*]I have documented the Savannah Bananas' growth trajectory in *Profit First*, *Clockwork*, and here in this book in chapter 7. The Bananas used Fix This Next to identify their greatest opportunity to date, and it is not what you think!

The results were remarkable. In a summer season when the average ticket (job) price declines due to overwhelming small-job repair demand, for the first time ever, IceBound increased their average ticket price from $7,300 to $12,500. This jump is unheard of in their industry—and it happened within four weeks! It took fifteen minutes to pinpoint the Vital Need and, after coming up with a fix, just four weeks not only to solve it, but to break industry records.

You need to do the same process for any Vital Need you resolve in your business, because numbers don't lie.

Fix It

As I was reading John Doerr's book, *Measure What Matters*, I was reminded of the simplicity and impact of measurements. Doerr calls them objectives and key results (OKRs). In other words, determine your goal (objective) and how you are going to measure your movement toward it (key results). Doerr goes on to explain how megacompanies such as Google and Intel used OKRs. The story that hit home with me was about Intel.

Intel identified a threat as Motorola started to gain ground in the CPU (central processing unit) market. Andy Grove, the president of Intel, responded with Operation Crush, a very simple plan to take back the market from Motorola. To track their progress, they put in a simple metric: units sold of the 8086 processor. Objective: beat Motorola. Key result: units sold of the 8086 CPU.

It's a simple equation, but the fascinating part is the strategy that came about. The commission-based salespeople were retrained to understand that while the money was not in the 8086, what it did do was lock the client in with Intel. The other technology they sold that supplemented the processor was where Intel (and the salesperson) made profit. Marketing strategies were developed. New education and marketing material was created, showing the benefits to the customer of Intel over Motorola. The plans were sorted out, the key result was tracked, and within less than a year Intel was king of the game again.

Metrics are the scoreboard. They are how you measure whether you are winning the game. Set up the scoring system, and the game reveals itself. No score, and you have no idea if you are winning or even if what you are doing is working.

Measurements are the scaffolding of the BHN. As you build your business, moving up and down the pyramid to strengthen the foundation and build out the higher levels, you will depend on the scaffolding—the things that give you access to the structure and put you in the right spot to build the structure correctly.

Once you identify your Vital Need within the BHN, you then build the scaffolding (measurements and tracking) around it to ensure you properly fix it. Specifically, I suggest you use a somewhat more comprehensive method than OKRs, a method that instills progress checkups and appropriate improvements in the objectives and measurements. I call it the OMEN method:

O—Objective. What is the result you intend to achieve?

M—Measurement. What is the most straightforward way to measure your progress toward your outcome?

▼
▼
▼
▼
▼

E—Evaluation. With what frequency will you analyze your measurements?

N—Nurture. If necessary, how will you tweak the objective and/or measurements?

1. *Objective:* What is the outcome you want to achieve for your Vital Need? Where does it currently stand (the baseline)? Identify the requirements for your goal to be considered successful and how you are going to move from your baseline to your objective.

2. *Measurement:* This includes the metric(s) for your outcome, within a specific time frame. What is the simplest way to effectively track your progress toward the objective? The fewer metrics the better. Minimize the number of metrics to avoid distraction and confusion, but have enough to give you an adequate reading of your progress.

3. *Evaluation:* Determine the frequency with which you will check your metrics and set interim goals on your way to the intended outcome.

4. *Nurture:* As you progress, you may notice that your objective isn't quite right or you aren't measuring it effectively. Make the objective and measurements highly visible/accessible to the relevant people. Then give you and your team permission to change the settings (objective, measurements, and/or evaluation frequency) to improve the progress toward the objective.

The OMEN method gives scrutiny and attention to the Vital Need you identified to resolve it as efficiently as possible. When the objective is achieved, you then remove the scaffolding of constant scrutiny and focus, and leave a key metric or two behind to ensure sustained results and signal if a new problem arises. Then move on to the next Vital Need and set up new scaffolding using OMEN. This is the building of a Dashboard, an important process I detailed in *Clockwork*.*

×

Now that I live by the BHN, I have the least stress I have ever experienced in my life. That doesn't mean I have no problems in my business; I constantly have challenges and problems and issues. Now, though, I know exactly what to do next: pinpoint the fix that will have the most impact and don't get distracted by the countless obvious but superficial issues.

When I complete the resolution to a current challenge, I go right back to the BHN to pinpoint exactly what I need to do next, regardless of all the urgent issues that constantly spring up. I wish I understood this a long time ago, and I'm glad to be able to help you understand this now. Because, you see, the only way to get unstuck quickly, to unlock a new level of growth for your business, is to stop wasting precious time and resources trying to fix the wrong problems, and instead zoom in on the right problem and fix it.

In the next five chapters, I'll go over each level of the BHN and help you zero in on your Vital Need. Addressing the Vital Need is the opportunity to strengthen your weakest link so that you can realize the vision you have for your company. You don't have to

---

*You can get the book and free resources at Clockwork.life.

carry around the secret about how frustrated you are with your business, or how long your business has been stuck at a plateau, or how your $22 million company is four weeks away from shuttering the doors. You don't have to live in fear that you may never make a go of it, that the naysayers in your life were right. Please don't let the good fortune of luck make you believe that success happened because of your skill, and please don't let your skills be discounted as luck. Take a breath and focus on what is *really* going on in your business. Pinpoint the most impactful issue. And then apply the fix.

Entrepreneurship is a challenge of epic proportion. You must build your wings only after you have made that leap of faith off the cliff. Whether you are years or decades into your journey, or even if this is day one, I know you're up for it. I am sure of this.

I know this, because even if you and I haven't met in person yet, we have something in common: the DNA of our businesses. Every business is built on the same DNA. It's only the choices we make that differentiate them. That's it. And with your new BHN compass, you will make different choices. Better choices. The *right* choices.

You were meant to avoid the boar paths of business and the oft-misguidance of your gut. You were meant for greatness. There is not one doubt in my mind. Grab your compass, my dear friend, we've got some business navigating to do.

TUNNEL VISION IS also a challenge for, well, all of humanity. But it can keep an entrepreneur stubbornly stuck in the same spot. We get frustrated because we are not seeing results, so we often respond by doing what's not working, only harder. This can be frustrating for people on the outside, because it is so obvious that tunnel vision is the problem. That is why I encourage you to engage the services of a qualified business coach. For decades I have employed business coaches to give me an outside perspective on my businesses, and I can't say enough positive things about the experience. In short, the good ones are trained to identify core challenges, giving guidance (or bringing in resources) to fix them, and are not emotionally attached to the business like you are. The Fix This Next model is an ideal way for you and your business coach to diagnose what your business needs next, and then you can get to it with your coach and fix it. Go to FixThisNext.com to get the free tools and coaching resources.

PERMISSION NOT TO READ

▼

▼

▼

Once you have pinpointed your Vital Need, flip to that level
and need in the following chapters. You don't have to read
the rest of this book to move your business forward.

Chapter 3

ESTABLISH PREDICTABLE SALES

WHEN I STARTED MY FIRST BUSINESS AT THE AGE OF TWENTY-three, I told myself, "When my company makes a hundred thousand dollars, I will be taking home a hundred thousand dollars." Boy, was I excited about that! I think I just heard you do a giggle-snort. I get it. I was naïve when I was starting out. I really believed that when a company makes money, the owner takes home basically the same amount. So that turned out to be bullshit.

I was in for a rude awakening when I actually managed to get the business to hit a hundred thousand in annual revenue and I was still turning out my pockets for spare change. I was far from making anything. I had to pull from my meager retirement fund to make payroll. I wasn't making a dime . . . yet. So I reasoned, "Ah, it must be at two hundred fifty thousand when you start making a decent take home." That benchmark came and went without a single increase in my personal income. I went from zero take-home to a big whopping zero in take-home. At that point, having already tapped my retirement account, I had to refinance my house for the first time to cover payroll. I then concluded that the magic number was five hundred thousand. When I hit that I would finally take home some good money and I would live the life of financial freedom. That turned out to be a myth, too, unless financial freedom means being free of having any money at all.

I continued my mind game. "It must all come together at a cool mil," I convinced myself. But to do that, I need a rainmaker. A hunter. A hot-shot salesperson so hungry for the sale they will do whatever it takes to get it. I figured most if not all of the problems we faced in my businesses could be fixed by increasing sales, so I focused on getting new work and new clients. My theory was bolstered by the fact that I actually liked talking about this aspect of my business. My ego was driven by two things: (1) bragging about the top line number: revenue, and (2) bragging even more about revenue.

After pushing hard to increase sales, I could finally brag that I had hit a million, I had refinanced my house yet again, and I had borrowed from friends to stay afloat. As my business grew to $2 million in annual revenue, and then $3 million, not only had my take home not really improved, it was more sporadic. The stress just multiplied. Holy crap, that stress! I became that weirdo you see in traffic jams, talking to himself in his car while randomly swatting at nonexistent flies. (Now I could be one of your bowling buddies.)

The truth is, your business will never take care of itself. Ever. The entrepreneur and the employees are the ones who must care for the business, to ensure it is built healthily from the foundation up. For the team to succeed, even if it is a team of one, we all must be moving toward a specific goal. And it all starts with *your* specific, *personal* goals. Not random sales targets, bragging rights, or trying to keep up with the Entrepre-Joneses.

After connecting with and/or speaking to well over one hundred thousand entrepreneurs over the past ten years, it has become clear to me that most of us have sales goals that are purely arbitrary. We pick a goal of five hundred thousand, or a million, or five hundred million out of the air, and then try to rally ourselves and our team to win. It's so random, it is like telling a Little League baseball team that they are going to win the Super Bowl by becoming champion drivers at the Indy. It sounds crazy big, but all it is, is big crazy.

It wasn't just that I set random goals and panicked to push for more and more sales; I also didn't have a clear understanding that the SALES level was not just about getting more clients, or more work from existing clients. I thought sales was simply about getting people to buy things, when that's actually just an itsy-bitsy part of it.

A sale is not a handshake or the swipe of a credit card. A sale is the creation and fulfillment of an agreement between you and your clients or customers. That agreement includes five distinct stages:

1. *The Connection:* This is the first part of the sales process, but you may think of it as what happens *before* the sale. In order for you to get clients to consider buying from you, you first have to make them aware that you exist, then help them see that you have a solution (your goods and/or services) that will help fulfill a need they have. If you are not authentic, consistent, and deliberate in your marketing, you may end up with clients you have no business serving, and that means

things can go haywire even before you "get the sale." The Connection phase is the sale before the sale.

2. *The Agreement:* Whether it's a contract, a receipt, some kind of blockchain record, an email, a handshake, or even huggin' it out, the agreement states the terms of the sale. In other words, the vendor (that's you) will provide specific goods, and the client typically gives the money in return.

3. *The Deliverable:* This is when the vendor (still you) completes the work or delivers the goods as promised to the client, within the time parameters and the "work standards" agreed upon.

4. *The Collection:* In this stage, the client pays the vendor (yay, you!) for the work or goods provided, within the time parameters and amounts agreed upon.

5. *The Conclusion:* This is when all agreed-upon terms are delivered and both parties confirm that all the parameters of the agreement are complete. This may also be when new terms are reached and the process starts again.

We all know we can't count those chickens until they hatch, and that we can't count on verbal offers; "nothin's nothin' until it's somethin'," and all that. But we do anyway. We feel the surge of dopamine when we get the handshake or fist bump or whatever. We feel exhilaration when the contract is signed. Of course, the sale is not complete yet, not until the cash is in the bank. However, even if you've collected the money, the sale still isn't complete. When you receive money from a client, it is not actually your money until you *earned* it—by doing the work to the level promised.

You may even have the client pay you prior to doing work. In this case, they are taking a risk giving you money with the expectation that you will do the work. If you fail to do the work, or fail to do it right, the money they gave you is not yours; it's still theirs. And you can't count those fluffy chickens until the agreement is fulfilled.

I realize this seems like basic stuff, but so few business owners learn this simple idea before it's too late. Technically, when you get money from a client, you are required to hold on to that money until the agreement is fulfilled or return the money if you don't deliver on your promise. How many of us actually do that? Not many. I sure didn't. Before I started implementing Profit First in my business, as soon as funds became available in my account, I was spending those dollars. Heck, it was already spent before I had gone and made the deposit . . . before I made the deal . . . in some cases, before I even knew how I would deliver on the deal.

Rainmakers are often focused on handshakes; they aren't thinking about the completion of the *entire* vendor-client agreement. When I had this realization, the idea of hiring a rock star sales team became less appealing to me. I didn't want someone who was on the hunt for the handshake, because I knew that they would dump overbloated promises on the service team, which would impact our ability to hold up our end of the agreement. It wasn't just the big guns who did this—I fell into the trap over and over again myself too. As the boss I could rationalize it, but let's be real: I was trying to get the sale (agreement), and figured we'd sort out the deliverables later.

This backfired on me in my first business, Olmec Systems. We installed computer systems for businesses, and in 2002, I noticed that VoIP phone systems were entering the market and were the opportunity of the future. With a VoIP phone, calls are sent and received over an IP network rather than a phone line. Seeing a future paved with gold, I contacted 3Com, who was one of the first major vendors to come out with a VoIP phone system. As the newest installer of 3Com VoIP systems, I landed a huge sale (the agreement part): a fifty-thousand-dollar, seventy-five-phone install for a company in New Jersey. Woo-hoo! That was a *big* number for me, and I was psyched.

I started imagining landing other big VoIP phone installs, and immediately declared Olmec a leading "VoIP vendor." I could foresee our bank account getting fatter, and any financial challenges we had disappearing with every deal. I was going to make it rain Grants and Franklins. (That's how us wannabe cool kids say fifties and hundreds.)

After I made the sale, 3Com called to tell me how excited they were to sell such a "big system." In fact, their exact response was, "That's a biiiig system. We can't believe it! Seventy-five? Holy shit," followed by a big pause and another, "Holy. Shit."

Their total shock and amazement should have been my first clue that disaster was on the horizon, but I was so enamored with the sale that I didn't see the red flags. Flags, *plural*. All the red flags. A whole warehouse full of big, bright red "holy shit" flags.

I soon found out that 3Com had never sold a system larger than five phones up to this point. *Five*. So they had no idea if a system of seventy-five phones could perform in the real world, as promised. (Spoiler alert: It couldn't.) Worse, we were in no position to install the system without guidance from 3Com, and after it was installed, we had no idea how to fix the countless problems that occurred on a daily basis.

Our fifty-thousand-dollar deal resulted in the client threatening to sue us, and we ended up cutting them back to their old system. We lost a lot of money, because we had to pay for all of our labor to install and uninstall the VoIP system, and to reinstall their original one, and *then* pay their old phone guy to fix the problems we ran into during the reinstall. It was months before we were able to get 3Com to agree to allow us to return their equipment and recoup some of our costs. We lost tons of time, tons of money, and worse than that, we lost *all* of our good reputation.

Obviously, this is one heck of a cautionary tale, but (1) it's true, and (2) it could most definitely happen to you if you or your sales team are focused more on the handshake than on whether or not you can execute on the sales agreement.

Sometimes, it's the client who doesn't hold up their end of the bargain, and a sale you put on the books as accounts receivable, that you counted on to keep the engine running, never material- izes. This isn't news to you; you've been there, done that, and al- ready used your "Been there. Done that. And all I got was this lousy T-shirt" T-shirt to wipe up that nasty mess. So why am I taking you back to Business 101? Because these are common problems that we accept as part of doing business, and yet the challenge you need to address *right now* so you can dynamite that plateau and move your business forward may have to do with one of the five sales stages.

I've found that the best salespeople are rooted in realism. They get clear on what truly serves their clients, and they are candid about their ability to deliver that to them. The best way to support a good sales team—even if that sales team is all you, Han Solo—is to get clear about your sales goals and why you set them, and ensure that every stage of the sales process is in tip-top shape.

Now let's go over the five Core Needs your company must meet in order to shore up the SALES level on the BHN.

Need #1: Lifestyle Congruence

Question: Do you know what the company's sales performance must be to support your personal comfort?

Of all the needs on this level, lifestyle congruence is one is the easiest and fastest to address, and brings great impact and clarity. Yet the majority of business owners I have met have not even considered how much income they need to take home in order to support their lifestyle. This is pillars in the ground, my friend. Without this, you are building on sandstone. This is fast and easy, but cannot be skipped.

I shared my own story at the start of this chapter, but I'm not alone; many businesses struggle with arbitrary goals. For example, a business may target $1 million in sales as their goal, and once that is surpassed, target $5 million, $10 million, or $100 million. Others will specify an arbitrary growth goal of 20 percent year over year. Or because they had 500 percent growth from one hundred thousand to five hundred thousand in one year, think they should have 500 percent growth for eternity. (Hint: You shouldn't; even your boy Jeff Bezos doesn't.) Setting an arbitrary sales goal is like setting a health goal of living one hundred and twenty years, yet ignoring the quality of life. You could reach the goal and still live a miserable life dealing with a lot of health issues.

For a business, the most overlooked yet simplest method for setting purposeful business goals is to tie them to personal significance. You need to be clear on the *personal* income that supports your current level of *personal* comfort as a starting point. Calculate how much you'll need—how much you'll *really* need. For many entrepreneurs, this means adequate income to support their current lifestyle and wipe out any current debt. It should also include a savings plan for future necessary expenses (such as buying a newer car, or saving for education or retirement). The goal here is to determine the "comfort number," not the "aspiration or dream income."

Once you've figured that out, reverse engineer the sales revenue you'll need to consistently support that. (I'll explain how to determine your take-home pay based on sales revenue below so you don't fall into the trap I did—growing sales but staying penniless.) You will set other goals, such as sales and profit targets, and number of employees. But they are all subservient to knowing what you need.

Many entrepreneurs falsely conclude that a bigger business is a better business. That is simply not true. The right-size business that provides you with comfort initially and the ability to grow personally in the way you desire and to increase your comfort is the better business. In other words, the goal is to have the right-size business for you.

Measurement is built right into this need. For you to know what the business needs, we need to know what *you* need. Remember, this is your comfort level (meaning you are not begging on the street), not your dream income—that will come in due course. First, add up your living costs. Then consider, and be truly honest with yourself, what are you willing to sacrifice in your personal life to reduce the cost burden to your company? You're probably used to giving stuff up to fund your business; you're a business owner, after all. When considering the sacrifices you're willing to make, think about how long you'd be willing to keep that up. Then determine how to do the numbers (the percentage of income that you will use for your compensation), what will bring the income levels to what you need, etc. The measurement is then super simple: Can you pay your personal monthly nut?

OMEN: Lifestyle Congruence

Let's pretend you've been in business for two years. You don't take a regular salary; instead, you withdraw money out of the business for yourself whenever you can. Your random income is hard to predict, so when you need more money for personal expenses, your solution has been to sell more and use the "backup" credit card yet again. Using this example, the OMEN process could go like this:

1. *Objective:* You want to make $150,000 a year. After addressing rent, food, utilities, and basic future savings, and cutting out luxuries such as the car lease and dinners out, you can live modestly yet comfortably on $100,000 a year. Your current annual take-home is roughly $45,000.

2. *Measurement:* Following the Profit First method of setting up bank accounts for different disbursements, you have set up an OWNER'S COMP account designated for your take-home pay. Let's say you decide to allocate 20 percent of your deposited revenue into OWNER'S COMP. To get to your goal of taking a $100,000 salary, your business would have to achieve $500,000 in annual sales. (Do you see how you don't need to sell millions to support your life?)

3. *Evaluation:* Assuming you process payroll every two weeks, you will review the two metrics (overall sales, your comp) biweekly. So you create a simple two-column spreadsheet that tracks sales and your salary, and calculates an average of the sales and salary to show the biweekly trend.

4. *Nurture:* Let's say you are the only one in charge of the company finances, so you will be the only one evaluating and making on-the-fly adjustments if deemed appropriate. You put a big sticky note above your desk that reads "Stay alive at the five," a reminder of your $500,000 annual sales goal. As you go through this process every two weeks, you know taking your salary is a good indicator in and of itself, so there is no need for tweaks for the measurements. However, you do notice an opportunity to tweak the plan. You can comfortably take 25 percent of sales as your owner's-comp allocation without adversely affecting the business. So you tweak the percentage to 25 percent and tie a new annual goal for lifestyle congruence at $400,000 in revenue. You change your sticky to now say "Life is not a bore when we hit the four!"

5. *Result:* You never expected that adjusting your lifestyle wouldn't compromise your happiness. It doesn't. Cool! Now you have a reason to hit $400,000 in sales, and it is not about being bigger or keeping up with the industry. Your sales goal directly relates to your own comfort, which is the secret sauce to future growth. No more desperate moves. No more selling just to sell. No more worrying about the Entrepre-Joneses. You have become more disciplined, more calculated, and the businesses foundation of your SALES level is stronger than ever as a result.

Need #2: Prospect Attraction

Question: Do you attract enough quality prospects to support your needed sales?

Once upon a time, I was that annoying "always-be-closing" cheese-ball every business owner hates: the guy who shows up unannounced to sell you something. You know, unsolicited soliciting. When I first started Olmec Systems, I got the brilliant idea to go door to random door selling our computer services. I was sure that my chiseled chin and charismatic personality would win over any business. (My wife was looking over my shoulder as I typed those words and is now in a heap on the floor in fits of laughter. I won't even charismatically turn my chiseled chin her way to acknowledge her.) So I set out on foot to try to land some clients.

I lasted one day. Actually, it was more like three hours. Door after door, I was either rejected or escorted out by security. After twenty-one consecutive rejections I sat on the sidewalk curb with drool dripping down my finely chiseled chin. Clearly, I didn't have a clue how to build awareness for my company, let alone how to attract the right customers for my business.

Most business owners go through three stages of awareness when it comes to finding clients or customers. First, there is the "anybody" stage, when you ignore your mom's warnings of "stranger danger" and think everyone in the world is a potential client. Next, you realize you are way off base, and you choose a market to sell to. This decision is usually based on what other businesses are doing, or not doing. Finally, you find *your* market—a market that serves your business. To find this market, you need to be clear about what your company can do, what your company wants, and what your company needs.

When prospects don't regularly identify your company as a solution to their needs, that means you are not "top of mind" with those prospects. By having a consistent presence in a community of ideal prospects, with a reputation for excellence, you will generate a degree of awareness in prospects, who will seek you out when they require your service or product. Look at any existing clients and identify the best ones. Which clients demonstrate that they value you? Which clients do you enjoy serving?

Prioritize the most significant attributes: for example, they *can* pay $10,000 in annual fees comfortably, because they have $1 million in revenue *and* they *want* to pay $10,000 in fees because they significantly value the time it saves them more than the fees. Identify other elements such as communication style, or their perception of the importance of your offering. What industry are they in? Or if you are a business-to-consumer company (B2C), what common demographics or psychographics do your customers share? Document the avatar and establish vetting questions around these elements.

Tersh and Julie Blissett of IceBound HVAC did this exact analysis. They determined that residential customers were better than commercial customers, because residential customers paid on time or in advance, while commercial customers stretched out the terms. Knowing this, Tersh and Julie identified the best existing residential customers: dual-income couples who value their time and whose kids were grown. These proved to be the best clients in Tersh and Julie's review of their sales history. With that, the new avatar was defined.

Then, seek out "congregation points." Where do they hang out? It could be that they attend conferences or are in the same club. They could be fans of a certain podcast or magazine. The goal is to find the places that your ideal avatars affirm and share their beliefs, experiences, and knowledge with others like them.

Take my wife, for example. She loves purses, shoes, and fashion in general. She also has a virtual congregation point with other like-minded ladies, a podcast called *My Favorite Murder*. She listens to it religiously. So does a tribe of hundreds of thousands of women who preach "Stay sexy and don't get murdered." They listen to the weekly show and have even adopted a tribe name: Murderinos. If you want to sell sexy purses and shoes or some pepper spray, you've found a congregation point for your target consumers. If you sell something else, you just need to ask where your own community of Murderinos hangs out and appear there.

Once you identify these communities, become an active participant. You can do this, in some cases, by just showing up or through PR (be the guest on the podcast), or by targeting marketing and advertising campaigns.

OMEN: Prospect Attraction

Let's say you have a web-design business. You create websites for dentists who want to optimize the number of leads their site captures. The Fix This Next analysis pinpointed your Vital Need as quality of prospects. Every dentist and their mother is calling you—literally. Last week, one dentist's mom called you because her "handsome son" needed a "professional inter-web-page" on "the Google" and she already has a design that she did in watercolor and needs you to build it, for five hundred dollars or less. Here's an example of how you might determine if you have shored up prospect attraction:

1. *Objective:* You need more quality prospects (including handsome mama's boy). In the past, you considered any prospect a good prospect, and the conversations you had with those prospects were mostly about negotiating your price. Once they became a client, half the time spent on calls was about how you executed your work, rather than going over the results you delivered. You now define a quality prospect by their willingness to pay your premium without squabbling over price, and they don't worry as much about what you do as what you deliver. You are aiming for 80 percent of your prospects to meet your quality standards; currently that number is at 50 percent.

2. *Measurement:* Rather than have several variables or custom fees, you set your per-project fee options as simple fixed numbers: $5,000 for a basic website, $7,500 for moderate upgrades, and $10,000 for advanced designs and functionality. You need regular inbound cash flow, so you may occasionally be flexible on price, but if the prospect is focused on getting a bargain, they are not quality. The other measurement of "micromanaging" is more qualitative, but you still find a way to put numbers to it. You track the ratio of questions your prospects ask about the execution of work, compared to the number of questions the prospects have about the outcome.

3. *Evaluation:* On average, your company lands about one client a week out of four prospects. So you decide that a good interval to check the accumulated data is once a month. This will give you enough "samples" to look at, roughly fifteen prospects considered each month. You create a simple three-column spreadsheet that your sales team manages. One column tracks a simple "Yes/No" answer to "Did the prospect ask for a price discount?" The second column reads: "Number of questions about our process?" The third column reads: "Number of questions about the outcome we deliver?"

4. *Nurture:* You work with your two salespeople who are handling all the inbound prospects on strategies to make your objective come alive. They suggest putting up a whiteboard to track the number of quality prospects that convert. Your salespeople give you the insight you have been waiting for: Fix your own website. Your website is beautiful, but it effec-

tively says, "We serve anyone." Now you have a plan to ensure your website says, "We serve specific people with specific needs." Sorry, handsome mama's boy.

5. *Result:* Your website redesign was key; the specificity about who you serve changed everything. Now you get fewer inbound inquires, but about 90 percent of them are from qualified dentists who are serious and ready to pay for a site that generates good leads for them. You achieved your quality prospect objective quickly, without needing to tweak the measurements. With this need addressed, you got back to the Fix This Next process to identify and fix the next Vital Need.

Need #3: Client Conversion

Question: Do you convert enough of the right prospects into clients to support your needed sales?

Garbage in, garbage out. In other words, the consistency of your input (leads) dictates the quality of your output (conversions). So once you strengthen the leads need, you will be in a better position to bolster conversions. Your business may need to ensure it is attracting quality prospects before focusing efforts on client conversion. Once you have a strong pipeline of quality prospects, the goal is to achieve a high conversion rate of those prospects, and if it applies to your business model, a high retention rate of those high-quality clients. In essence, you will serve fewer types of clients better by doing fewer things better.

If you are spending significant time on prospects who don't become clients, or become clients but of low quality, you may be dealing with one or more of the following issues:

1. A problem with the prior needs, such as lifestyle congruence: selling to just sell. Or a problem with prospect attraction. For example, providing incentives for bringing on any client versus a good client.

2. An unclear or nonexistent definition of a good client, or failure to qualify prospects against those parameters. Selling the wrong thing the right way or selling the right thing the wrong way: this is like selling ice to Eskimos; they just don't need it. Even if you are the "greatest salesperson in the world" and "can sell ice to Eskimos," you are still selling the wrong thing. Which, I guess, means you're not the best salesperson in the world.

   When you sell the right thing the right way, you are speaking to the customers' true needs. Customers don't buy features; they buy benefits. Tersh sells to people who want a comfortable home year-round (benefit) and don't want to oversee the work (benefit).

3. Overpromising is selling more than you can deliver. It's basically the same as lying, except said with kindness and, possibly, cluelessness. I was a client for a project for which we were buying knives. The vendor's salesperson promised, "We will deliver these on time, every time, even if I need to make the knives myself. Mark my word." They didn't deliver and he didn't make the knives. The next order came up

and I heard the same overpromise, which was a red flag that nothing had improved. We canceled the order and moved on with an alternative.

4. Overselling is the trap of explaining more and more about your offering when the customer has already made a decision to buy from you. The thing is, while you are trying to get the sale, people flip-flop between "I should do this" and "I shouldn't do this." The more you explain, the more details you ask them to consider, which pushes them to flop to a no decision, or to postpone making a decision.

5. Filtering in as opposed to filtering out. This is when you try to make the prospect a fit by looking for indications that you should work with them. Filtering out is when you look for any indication of why they are *not* a fit, and is a more stringent and effective approach for selecting ideal prospects.

Conversion is a consideration of both sides: What do *they* want and what do *you* want. Too often, businesses just focus on what *they* want and do whatever it takes to "get the yes."

My old-school mentality was always: get prospects to say yes. But then I discovered the better question to ask is: How do I make myself say yes? Meaning, how do I know I can and want to serve these people? I focused on what would make prospects a good fit for my business, not the other way around.

The key is to ensure that you and your client are in alignment. Do you get the most joy out of selling on price, convenience, or quality? What type of clients will be a joy for you to serve? What services or products are a joy to deliver? Once you have figured out this point, you have found your "it." Then ask these simple questions:

Is my company story consistent with it?

Is my pricing consistent with it?

Is the experience I deliver consistent with it?

The definitive source for the way to engage prospects and convert them to clients is Donald Miller's book, *Building a Story Brand: Clarify Your Message So Customers Will Listen*. I thought I had a handle on how to do this—until I met "the Don." I always thought that as an entrepreneur, the role of my company was to be the hero, swooping in to rescue the customer from whatever sticky situation they were stuck in. Don taught me that instead I needed to treat my clients as the hero and consider myself their guide. Your client is Luke Skywalker, not you. You are Obi-Wan Kenobi.

First, examine your incentives for bringing on clients. If you have a sales team, are they rewarded for closing clients or are they rewarded for the longevity and quality of the client? Or do you give recognition for quantity of sales versus quality, such as a metric board that measures number of clients instead of happiness of clients or longevity of clients?

OMEN: Client Conversion

Let's say you just bought an auto repair shop. The business has been around for decades and has a great reputation around town. You ran the FTN analysis on the business after you acquired it and saw a massive variety in clients. Foreign cars, domestic cars, exotics, motorcycles, ATVs, and even a few mountain bikes have been serviced at this place last month. This business has the mentality that any customer is a good customer, but you know that is not true. The variety of customers imposes a massive variety of requirements on your new business. The more variety of demand on your business, the weaker it is. You are going to make your auto shop rock solid by serving only your best customers.

1. *Objective:* You want more of the right customers to use your shop. Your team, and your interests, are with domestic cars. Currently only 25 percent of your business is domestic automobile repair. Your objective is to have 51 percent of your work be domestic repair.

2. *Measurement:* Sometimes the compensation structure for sales individuals is not tied to quality of customer. Consider commissions or reward structures that value longtime, high-quality customers. Consider rewarding the conversion of prospects that most closely match the avatar of the ideal client. Consider diminished rewards for prospects who become customers but don't match the avatar. The first thing you define is the time frame for that goal: you want domestic repairs to reach 51 percent within one year. Next, you track the number of domestic jobs per week. You were doing about four domestic jobs per week before, and you can meet your objective if you increase that number to ten per week.

3. *Evaluation:* You schedule yourself to review the numbers every Friday. You already have a minisocial for your team on Fridays at closing time. Now you will add a brief, informal meeting to discuss the progress on your Objective.

4. *Nurture:* You meet with your repair techs to explain the goal and how it will benefit them. They can concentrate on their mastery of specific skills, they can get more training, and you can even have some of the vendors of domestic car parts strike special deals with the shop. One mechanic raises her hand to share an idea: to use an old-school blackboard and, with chalk, mark off each domestic job they did that week.

   On Friday, when you close the shop at 5:00 p.m., you all have a beer together and discuss the board. The first month, it's just numbers, but it does show that you consistently get four jobs or so a week. Then the ideas start percolating. What about gifting new domestic car customers with "Made in America" stickers and hats? What about giving prospects with domestic cars expedited services when they become a customer? What about . . . ?

5. *Result:* With the OMEN in place, the right prospects take notice immediately and the special treatment of domestic prospects starts to yield a turn. Within three months, the domestic job frequency is now five per week, and within a year you are at nine a week. Not exactly what you hoped, but damn close.

Need #4: Delivering on Commitments

Question: Do you fully deliver on your commitments to your clients?

Every year, the financial news site 24/7 Wall St. publishes their list of the twenty most hated companies in America. On past lists you'll find companies such as United Airlines, Facebook, Equifax, Uber, and the Weinstein Company. I suspect you probably don't have to read the annual roundup to figure out why these companies suck. What all of these companies have in common is that their customers feel they let them down. Whether they didn't keep customer info safe, or sold it to the highest bidder; whether they mistreated employees or engaged in criminal behavior; whether they overpromised and underdelivered on products and services, all of these companies lost their way . . . and some of the customers.

I have a simple rule that has saved my business from being the twenty-first most hated company: "No news is still news." We're told "no news is good news" when it comes to customer feedback, because that means they're happy with their experience with your company. I don't subscribe to that. No news could mean that a client just doesn't want to tell you they're *unhappy*. Many people avoid confrontation like the plague, and those people are not going to tell you when they are miserable, or pissed, or both. Instead, they'll quietly give their business to your competitor, leaving you to wonder what happened. The key to killing it in the delivery phase of the sales agreement is setting expectations and beating them, or resetting them when you fall short. No matter if you can deliver on your promise as expected or you've fallen behind, keep your customer informed of your progress *before* they are compelled to inquire.

If you're not delivering for your clients as promised, it might be because you are caught in what Barry Moltz and Mary Jane Grinstead, authors of *B-A-M! Bust A Myth: Delivering Customer Service in a Self-Service World*, call the double-helix trap. This is when your company's focus oscillates between sales and deliverables. You need sales to fuel your business, and then you have to deliver on those sales agreements. The challenge is, many entrepreneurs only focus on *one or the other*. When there are no sales agreements to fulfill, your team shifts to signing more work. When the sales come in, your attention is now on delivering on those agreements. But once you take your attention off sales, you start to notice business slowing down, so you have to shift your focus back to sales to keep the engine running, which means you fall short on delivering as promised. If this problem is left unaddressed, this back-and-forth will result in team and owner burnout, loss of clients, and possibly loss of reputation. You may not become the most hated company in your industry, but you could come close.

A delivery challenge could also mean that you are simply maxed out on deliverables, which can happen to seasonal companies, such as tax accountants or snowplow folks, and to any company that is going through a big sales launch. If your business is in this position, it points to an inefficiency within the deliverable process. Inevitably, there will be a bottleneck within the production process that needs to be opened. Instead of trying to increase efficiency in multiple areas, focus on the biggest bottleneck (the area where the most work piles up and waits for the bottleneck to process it) and find improvements so you can eliminate it. This may involve identifying redundancies in equipment, staff, or both. Or you may need to redesign and streamline the way the bottlenecked process is completed. If you are a solopreneur, the fix might be to hire someone to execute on deliverables for you so you can focus on higher-impact tasks.

OMEN: Delivering on Commitments

For this OMEN example, let's imagine you have a dog-walking business. You are great at getting new clients, but your Fix This Next analysis defined the Vital Need that you need to fix immediately if you are going to sustain a healthy foundation for your business. You aren't delivering on commitments consistently. In fact, your online reviews are not too flattering.

1. *Objective:* You see from the reviews the complaints are consistently about scheduling. "They said they would be here at 8:00 a.m. and arrived at 8:40 a.m. I had to stay here with my dog until they arrived, and I was late for work as a result. This company sucks!" As your mom taught you, a minute late is still late, so you use that as the definition for late. Historically, your dog-walking team has arrived late about 60 percent of the time. Your objective is to be on time 98 percent of the time. You acknowledge that perfection is impossible, since your team is subject to factors outside their control. Foul weather, for example, can really foul up scheduling.

2. *Measurement:* The measurement is simple: did your team arrive at a client site at the scheduled time or earlier? You just need one metric, on time or not (defined by greeting the customer at the designated arrival time or up to five minutes prior). Since your team doesn't want to disappoint you, they will of course try their best, but they may also bend the truth a little. So you set up an enforcement system, a daily three-

question client survey that includes the question: Were we on time?

3. *Evaluation:* You have more than one hundred active clients, and most require daily visits on weekdays. This allows you to collect a lot of good data and gives you the ability to check it daily.

4. *Nurture:* The team meeting doesn't go as planned. Everyone knows they need to be on time, every time. They are already working their butts off to get all the work done. So while they all agree that you nailed the metric, the fix requires a team brainstorm to find a way to pull this off. Someone says, "How about we underpromise and overdeliver?" explaining that you could shift from exact appointment times to half hour arrival-time windows. Instead of saying you will arrive promptly at 9:00 a.m., you'd say, "We are scheduled to arrive between 8:45 a.m. and 9:15 a.m." Now your team has the flexibility they need to account for fluctuations in their day. The team also gives you active feedback on your metrics and discovers there is a different definition of late. Even when a walker arrives early, if the homeowner doesn't know they are there, the homeowner may still feel the walker is late. So the new measurement is acknowledgment of an early arrival by texting the owner when they pick up their dog.

5. *Result:* Clients are thrilled. Within a month of implementation of the new plan, and with only minor tweaks, your metric puts you at a 99 percent on-time arrival rate. Clients loved the texts notifying them the walker was at the house because you accompanied the notifications with impromptu

selfies of your dog walker with Fido. Who knew all it took was to change the client's perception of on time? Well, you and your team did.

Need #5: Collecting on Commitments

Question: Do your clients fully deliver on their commitments to you?

At my company, Profit First Professionals, we ring a massive gong when a new member signs up. That means we are in step two of the sales agreement process, and that is a milestone worth celebrating. In the past, I would mentally count the money as earned as soon as the contract was signed. So when I looked at my accounts-receivable report and saw the money owed to me, I thought of it as money that would soon be in my bank account. If the number was high, I felt good, because I assumed it was money I would eventually get. Except, sometimes, clients didn't pay. Other times, they didn't pay in full.

By leaving the responsibility of accounts receivable to my team, I made it their issue, when it was really part of the sales process. Yes, at times you need to enforce collections on a client because they are not fulfilling their obligation. But other times, you are not fulfilling yours.

It never feels good to be owed money. As I explained earlier, a sale is only truly complete once both sides have delivered on the agreed-upon terms, which includes the client paying in full, on time.

To resolve a collections issue, you could:

1. Change (and enforce) the terms to require payments earlier, or in larger amounts up front.

2. Offer alternative payment methods, such as payment by credit card, putting the responsibility on the lender to get the funds.

3. Offer alternative methods that make it more convenient for clients to pay, such as PayPal or Zelle.

4. Implement a collections plan, for example: request confirmation of receipt of invoice and send a notification when a bill is almost due.

5. Track individual client collections and put restrictions and/or requirements on poor-paying customers.

If your agreement is that the client pays you a certain amount by a certain time, and they are not fulfilling that, you have a sales problem. If you tolerate it, you have become a bank (lender) to your client, and I highly suspect that you don't own a bank. If you don't tolerate it, you are managing your sales need properly.

A factor that comes into play is the Borrower/Lender Obligation Matrix, which mirrors the vendor-client relationship. As a new relationship turns into an ongoing one, the sense of obligation for you (the lender, in this scenario) and the customer (the borrower) changes. At the start of a new relationship the borrower has a heightened sense of obligation to pay the lender back, because of the "high" they feel from the acquisition of the goods or the receipt of a loan.

Over time, though, the borrower's sense of obligation to pay the lender back decreases. Their focus shifts to other things, the "high"

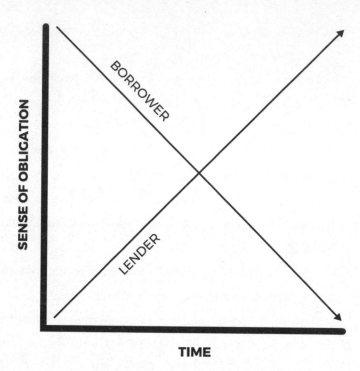

Figure 5. Borrower/Lender Obligation Matrix

of the initial transaction fades, and they move on to other purchases they need to make. Conversely, each day without payment increases the lender's sense of obligation. Now the lender becomes concerned about getting—or not getting—paid. As time passes, the responsibility shifts from the borrower's sense of obligation to pay back, to the lender's ability to collect what is owed. Since you are the lender, time is *not* to your advantage, pal.

From a lender's point of view—again, that's you—you want to put a tighter time frame on payment terms. Even small payments made frequently can serve both the borrower and the lender, because it keeps the borrower's payment obligation heightened and, because regular payments are being made, it decreases the lender's collection obligation.

If you pinpoint that collections are the Vital Need you must address next, I strongly encourage you to make collecting on old delinquent debt part of your plan.

Zach Smith's former company, Analog Method, had a twenty-five-thousand-dollar past-due account with a company that made school meals. Every month, Zach would call and ask for the bill to be paid in full, and they would say they couldn't afford it. The debt was nearly one year past due, and the Borrower/Lender Obligation Matrix had set in deeply.

I suggested a simple change to Zach's plan. The next time he called, he asked his customer, "What can you reasonably afford to pay weekly?"

"We don't know," they replied.

"Can you pay a penny?" Zach asked.

"Yes, of course."

"A dollar?"

"Absolutely."

"What about fifty dollars?" Zach pressed.

"Sure."

"One hundred?"

"Yeah, that wouldn't be a problem."

"How about two hundred fifty?"

The customer replied, "Probably not."

Now Zach had a range of how much his long-delinquent customer could comfortably pay. "Would you be able to pay back two hundred each week? Would that hamper you in any way?" he asked.

"No, it wouldn't. We could pay that."

"Okay. Two hundred a week it is."

We got Zach's customer on a rhythm of paying; the amount didn't really matter. From that moment on, Analog Method was back on their radar weekly. They had shifted the Borrower/Lender Obligation Matrix back in their favor. The client no longer thought of that bill as one they "couldn't pay," because we found the amount they *could* pay. The debt was now top of mind for the customer and their sense of responsibility to pay it off was reinstated. Some weeks, if they could afford it, they even paid way more than the two hundred. It took another year, but the entire twenty-five thousand was paid back in full.

For the past four years, Cyndi Thomason, the founder of the bookkeeping firm bookskeep, has been a willing early adopter of the new concepts I write about. She was one of the first companies in the world to become certified in Profit First, used the niche growth method I detail in my book *Surge** to grow her business from less than $50,000 in annual revenue to nearly $1 million, and used the Clockwork process to streamline her business so that she could take her first annual four-week vacation. (She and her husband just got back from their second four-week vacation as I write these words. Great pics, Cyndi!)

Cyndi had a meeting with her team to address the pain and overwhelm from growing so quickly. For a bookkeeping firm, an additional $250,000 of revenue each year, over four years, represents *a*

Surge and the accompanying free resources can be found at SurgeByMikeMichalowicz .com.

lot of additional obligation. At the meeting, Cyndi asked everyone on the team to do the Fix This Next analysis. They agreed on many points and differed on others, which resulted in an insightful discussion.

There is power in perspectives. As the business owner, you can do the Fix This Next analysis by yourself, for sure. But to really amplify the tool, do the analysis with your team and a business coach.*

The bookskeep team identified needs on multiple levels, including a challenge on delivering on commitments and a capacity issue at the SALES level, a challenge with minimized wasted effort at the ORDER level, and a challenge around mission motivation at the IMPACT level, among other things.

They followed the golden rule of the FTN analysis and determined the *biggest* need at the *lowest* level, which was delivering on commitments at the SALES level, thereby identifying their Vital Need.

Occasionally, when you tackle a problem that addresses a Vital Need, you'll end up fixing two for one. For example, in trying to solve the problem so bookskeep could say with confidence that they delivered on commitments, they ended up fixing another unchecked need in the ORDER level: linchpin redundancy. Here's how that happened: Cyndi and her team realized that they needed to take a look at where their flow of work slowed down. Everyone at bookskeep has a specific ability, but no two people have the same ability. Meaning, if one person was unavailable or couldn't keep pace with

---

*Visit FixThisNext.com to find a business coach who is certified in the Fix This Next process.

their work, no one else could do it. Everyone dependent on that work would need to wait until that person returned or caught up.

Because work comes in surges, at any given time one person would be overwhelmed, leaving everyone else effectively twiddling their thumbs because they couldn't help and missing deadlines as a result.

To solve the problem, first bookskeep trained staff in the core skills so they could do one another's work, allowing a team to tackle an overflow of work that was once contingent upon one person. Employees still played to their strengths and skill sets, but now there was overflow redundancy in place. Cyndi also hired a "floater," a person whose sole job was to fill in wherever the company needed extra capacity at the moment; this person went through the most in-depth training. The day this was implemented bookskeep took another giant leap forward in its growth. They were back to delivering on commitments (SALES), and as a bonus linchpin redundancy was in place (ORDER). Two birds, one stone.

Remember, after you fix what's next, your most Vital Need, you repeat the Fix This Next process by analyzing the BHN from the bottom up. When bookskeep ran the analysis again, they discovered the new Vital Need on the ORDER level (minimized wasted effort) and are tackling it as I write this.

OMEN: Collecting on Commitments

For this next scenario, let's say you own a photography studio. You are known for your family portraits. On average, customers pay twenty-five hundred dollars for the shoot, edits, prints, and framing.

It's a nice business, except people aren't paying you on time. Or ever. Time for the OMEN:

1. *Objective:* Currently only half of your customers pay within your 30-day terms, and 10 percent of clients never pay you at all. Sure, they don't get the prints, but you spent all that time doing the studio shoot and editing and got squat as a result. You want 100 percent of clients paying on time within the next month, or it's just not worth it to keep going.

2. *Measurement:* This one is simple. You will just track one metric: collections. You expect to have zero accounts receivable.

3. *Evaluation:* You have many clients in process right now, so you can't expect change overnight. You do 150 of these shoots a year, with about 125 of them happening during the busy holiday season, which is about six months away. So you will track the results on a monthly basis and plan to update your objective completely in nine months, after holiday season.

4. *Nurture:* You teamed up with your husband in your photography business. You do the pics, he does the books. He makes a simple but scary suggestion: request the entire payment up front! That would solve everything, but will your customers jump ship? The reason you gave 30-day terms in the first place was to attract new customers away from your competition, who offered payment plans. But attracting new customers means nothing if they don't pay. You are known regionally

as the best for family portraits, so you bite your tongue and say, "Let's do it."

5. *Result:* Ends up people weren't bad at paying you; they were bad at budgeting. After the photo shoot and while you were working on the editing of pictures, their holiday bills poured in. They would get swamped with expenses that they neglected to account for, and you were last (or never) on their list. Only a handful of clients were "surprised" that you required full payment up front. Everyone else just paid up front because you asked. The fact that you take credit cards makes it easy for your customers to pay you. And if they can't pay their credit card bill, that is the credit card company's issue, not yours. Your accounts receivable dropped to zero within nine months, because if people didn't pay up front you would not proceed. Not that you were a scrooge, you just didn't want to be screwed. You're taking hubby out for dinner tonight!

Fix This Next in Action

Jacob Limmer owns two boutique coffee shops, Cottonwood Coffee. He also has a roastery (a coffee-roasting facility). When I met with Jacob, he said, "I hate the name roastery; I use it because it's quick and easy. I also hate it when people throw in the superfluous 'e' in words such as fair, old, and town to make it faire, olde, and towne." No wonder I love this guy. I'm a sucker for weirdo observations.

Working through the SALES level, Jacob realized he had to address the Vital Need: lifestyle congruence. He figured he needed to clear and take home four thousand dollars a month from his stores. That number is for what he calls "Midwest comfort." He can live on that and not worry about putting food on the table. He won't be rich, but he won't panic about making a dollar the next morning.

Jacob told me, "I felt proud. My ego told me I don't need to be at the very beginning of the BHN tool. I have been in business for thirteen years. I wanted to resist the truth that the BHN revealed. I thought I was beyond this. But busting my ass for thirteen and a half years and not even taking home four thousand dollars a month is a 'what the hell' kind of moment. The BHN made me face a truth that I denied for years. I then spent an afternoon getting clear on what I really needed to not worry about my day-to-day living. And with that, I instantly could figure out what I needed from the business."

When you have clarity about how much you need to support your lifestyle, setting sales goals is super easy. It's the first Core Need I shared with you for a reason, because without this understanding, your business is a house built on a vague idea rather than a hard truth. That said, while you always start at the bottom level of the BHN and work your way up, you don't have to work through the Core Needs in sequence *within* that level.

In the next chapter, I'll share the shocking discovery Jacob had when he moved on to the PROFIT level. I love a good cliffhanger.

Chapter 4

CREATE PERMANENT PROFIT

PROFIT IS THE ONE CONCEPT COMMONLY MISUNDERSTOOD BY EN-trepreneurs. Generating profit isn't about making money for your business; it's about *taking* money *from* your business. Here's how I define profit: cold hard cash that the shareholder(s) (the owner or owners of the business) can use for themselves in any way they want, such that using it will not negatively impact the continued healthy operations of the business. If you want to use your profit to save for your future or wipe out personal debt, you can do that. Or if you want to spend your profit on a sweet motorcycle and then ride that beauty off into the sunset, you can do that too.

Ford recently sent me a check for $13.23. As I am a shareholder of a little less than one hundred shares, every quarter Ford sends a profit distribution check to me and all the other stockholders. I didn't take that check and say, "Oh shucks, Ford needs this more than I do. Let me return the money so Ford can use it to grow their business." And I didn't say, "I better get on over to the factory and work the line for a little bit to earn this money." What I did do was blow it on a killer large cheese pizza. If Ford had had a better quarter, I could even have gotten some sweet toppings.

Investors take risks. The stock value can go up or it can go down. The check for thirteen dollars and change was a reward for the risk I took as a shareholder in Ford. You are a shareholder, too, in your business. Chances are you probably own a massive percentage of stock in your own company—you may own 20 percent, 50 percent, or maybe even 100 percent. Profit is a reward for the tremendous risk you have taken on as an investor. When profit comes out, you (the shareholder) take it. It is your company thanking you for taking the risk to start it and keep it running. And we, as members of the global economy, thank you for the extraordinary work you are doing to participate in it.

To be clear, reinvesting profits into your business means it is *not* a profit and it *never* was. Say it with me: Ploughing back profit means it is *not* a profit. Never was and never will be. A reinvestment of "profit" is an expense. Period.

For example, I was speaking to an entrepreneur who told me she had a 22 percent profit that year but reinvested it all in the business. She was boastful of the profit her business achieved. Being a little bit of a judgy-judge, I burst her bubble.

I asked her, "Did the business spend that reinvested profit?"

She said, "Yes! We found a way to use every penny."

I explained, "If you spend money, it is an expense. Plain and simple. Just because you called it profit for a period of time, and then the business spends it, does not make it a profit." Never was. Never will be.

Don't let accounting terms confuse you. If the business spends money it is an expense. And don't try to soften the blow by calling it a reinvested profit. Only if the cash stays put in the bank or gets distributed to a business's shareholders is it profit.

Many business owners believe that they would be profitable if they could just increase their sales. They keep trying to sell more and more, hoping profit will magically appear. It won't. The truth is, sales do not translate to profit. The reason is that we're human. We spend what we have. So no matter how much we bring in, unless we are focused on profit *first*, we will continue to struggle to be profitable.

Your business can be permanently profitable from your very next bank deposit if instead of waiting to see what income you have left over after paying all your bills, you simply take out the profit first.* When you take a set percentage off the top of every deposit and move it into an account specifically reserved for profit, this forces you to streamline your expenditures. The full system is documented in *Profit First*, and involves setting up multiple accounts into which you disburse percentages of your income, but the core insight is to take your profit from every sale and be automatically forced to adjust your business properly to support that profit.

Readers, colleagues, and clients who follow this system have managed to transform their businesses from zero profitability to sustainability to thriveability in very short order. That's what we're focused on at this PROFIT level, folks. *Sustainability and thriveability*. Without profit, your company will be stuck constantly teetering on the edge of going under.

One of the most devastating days in my entrepreneurial career

---

*If you've read *Profit First*, you know this concept well.

was when I had to lay off nearly half of my employees. My partner and I had grown our forensic business to $3 million in annual revenue in two years and we were on a trajectory to more than double in our third year, yet we struggled to cover payroll every month. I had a habit of hiring too many people and paying them too much; I got a big ego boost out of saying that we had thirty employees.

The hardest person to face during the layoffs was not someone I actually let go—my personal assistant, Patti Zanelli. On the day I had to fire people, I brought everyone into a room and started to explain what was going on. Within a minute of me saying, "I will have to let go . . ." Patty's eyes welled up with tears. She stood up and quickly walked out the door. That was the moment I realized I had built a family—a business family—on quicksand. I hadn't built the foundation to support us, and I had hired a bunch of people before shoring up the critical needs that should have come first.

In that moment, I wanted to blame the economy, or our competition, or the fact that we had had a bad sales month. All those things were true, but none of these issues were the root cause of the problem. The real issue was my ignorance about how money really worked. Ever since we opened our doors, I had turned a blind eye to the finances and "left it to my partner." It certainly wasn't his fault because I wasn't paying attention.

So I had to fess up. I scanned the expectant faces of our employees and said, "I screwed up. Royally. We don't have enough money to stay in business as we are. My lack of leadership put us in this position. I have to let people go today, not because of you, but because of me. We need to get back to a size that will allow us to survive, a size that we can sustain. If we don't, we'll have to close."

At this point, tears were streaming down my face. All that was left to say was, "I am sorry. I am so sorry. This has been the hardest decision of my life."

I let twelve people go that day. We went from thirty employees to eighteen, and then I called in the remaining staff and made the biggest rookie mistake you can make after firing nearly half of your company: I told the remaining people that I needed them more than ever, but to keep them I needed to cut their salaries by 10 percent across the board. Ugh. I still groan when I think about that error in judgment.

What I *should* have done was laid off one or two more people so that I could keep the remaining team at full salary. You see, when you lay people off and cut salaries, those who made the cut get scared. They think their jobs are in jeopardy. Because I cut their salaries *after* laying people off, they assumed I hadn't fixed the business. This was the trigger for them to start quietly looking for new jobs.

Three weeks after the layoffs, we landed a major project that brought in tons of cash flow. Immediately, I reinstituted everyone's full salary with back pay, but the damage had been done. People kept looking, and I lost some key people as a result. And you know what? They were right to leave, because I *hadn't* fixed the company. We just landed a crucial sale. It took me multiple financial train wrecks to understand that I needed a better system, and that I couldn't sell my way out of every problem. If I had mastered the PROFIT level, many of the heartbreaks I experienced never would have happened.

You see, when you master the PROFIT level you bring fiscal

health to your company. You reserve money for profitability, you accumulate cash reserves for emergencies, and you stay within the confines of what you truly can afford. That includes paying employees. Instead of overstaffing, when I mastered PROFIT I knew what I truly had to spend and hired within those parameters. When I had a bad month or quarter my cash reserves could cover payroll while I strategically planned our route to get back on track.

Profit is a necessary foundation for any healthy business. It is also a reward for taking on risk. According to the 2016 Global Entrepreneurship Monitor (GEM) United States Report released by Babson College, 25 million Americans were running businesses that year, which means roughly 7.7 percent of the U.S. population are entrepreneurs. The fact that *you* own a business puts you in an elite group of risk-takers. Ninety percent of the population will never take on the challenges you've taken on. Ninety percent of the population will never follow through on their business ideas. Ninety percent of the population will not have the courage to show up every day and try to make something out of nothing. You are a superhero, and your profit distributions are a reward for your courage, for your risk-taking, and for providing jobs to the other 90 percent of us.

In this chapter, I'll share the five needs your company must meet in order to shore up the PROFIT level on the BHN before you can focus on the next level. Your industry and/or your business may have specific PROFIT-related needs not mentioned below, but trust the process and focus on the five Core Needs described below *first*. You might be surprised to discover that the other needs are resolved in the process. And when you've fixed your next problem, go back to the BHN compass and start over again. Always go back to the base level, SALES, and work your way up.

Need #1: Debt Eradication

Question: Do you consistently remove debt rather than accumulate it?

Before I implemented the process of taking my profit first in my business, I was drowning in debt. I remember listening to the radio as I was driving home from a meeting, when a commercial caught my attention. The announcer said, "The average American has seven thousand dollars of personal debt." I remember repeating in my head, *I want to be average. I want to be average.*

I had built and sold two multimillion-dollar companies, and within three years, lost every dime I earned due to my ego and my arrogance. I had decided I was a business wunderkind, and that I would be the best damn angel investor of all time. Instead, I ended up leveraged to the hilt and ultimately lost it all.

At the time I heard the commercial, I had about $75,000 in credit card debt, and I owed one of my friends $35,000. I also had a $250,000 SBA loan that I maxed out in one year; I couldn't make the minimum payments. Earlier that week, another friend wrote me a check for $3,000 to help me cover rent and groceries for the next few months. Every day, I received calls and letters from companies that "fix debt" problems. I know, they sound like the mob. And since I live in New Jersey, they quite well could have been the mob. Now that I think about it, there was one debt fixer who promised to consolidate my debt and get debt forgiven, so "you don't need to worry abowdit, Mikey Pal." Pretty sure *that* was the mob.

After I confessed my failures to my wife and kids, my nine-year-old daughter, Adayla, offered up her piggy bank to help me out. I had never been lower—financially or emotionally—and it forced me to take a hard look at my choices and my rationalizations.

At the opening of this chapter I gave you props for being a risk-taker and for having the courage to start your own business. I meant that. However, that same drive within us can also get us into a lot of hot water. We tell ourselves that we'll be able to "turn things around" with the next big sale, or next quarter, or next year, and justify accumulating mounds of debt. Whether it's ego or a generally hopeful and positive outlook on life, we tend to rack up personal and business debt in anticipation of something coming to fruition.

When a business requires accumulating debt to cover its expenses, it is experiencing "upside-down" cash flow, and the runway for the company's ability to sustain gets shorter. Remember this simple rule: *When you can't pay your bills, you can't afford your bills.* Period. If you are not able to pay your bills without incurring debt, your basic PROFIT-level needs are not being met.

If this is true for your business, the actions to take are twofold:

1. Cut costs.
2. Increase margins.

The first step to cut costs is to stop incurring new debt. To do this, analyze your current spend within the business as well as how much the owners need minimally to draw—the true minimum draw to survive, not some lame-o "but I need to keep my Tesla" number. Then use a "rip off the Band-Aid" approach to immediately cut all costs down to the minimum possible.

A simple but effective rule of thumb is to first determine what your monthly spend is and then multiply that by 10 percent. Then, endeavor to immediately cut that cost from your business permanently so that by the next month, you will have an ongoing 10 percent savings. Then repeat the process of calculating the new monthly nut and cut that by 10 percent. A business can only cut so much cost before it causes irreparable damage, but at the same time, maintaining costs that the business cannot afford triggers the most damage to the business (and possibly to the owners with their personal guarantees). Cut the fat, not the muscle.

Cutting costs would be easy and quick if it weren't for the humanness in all of us. We justify our spending and cling on to things we already possess. I remember an entrepreneur (who will remain nameless) who asked me to spend a day with him at his California office to help him figure out why his multimillion-dollar distribution business was financially struggling. When I arrived, he picked me up at the airport in his brand-new Audi R8. If you don't know what that is, one hundred eighty-five thousand George Washingtons can show you.

On arrival, I could already show him an adjustment he could make that would put the business on the right course: ditch that car. When we dug into the business later that day, there were dozens of other R8 types of opportunities. He was selectively blind to all of them, because you can't see the business from the outside when you are on the inside. You, too, will benefit from the services of a coach who can see what you can't.*

As I said, I once had a habit of hiring too many people at too-high salaries. Over time, I developed a strategy for determining if I could afford to hire an employee well before I posted the job vacancy. First, I determined the type of compensation I would pay. Then I set up a new account called FUTURE EMPLOYEE and started allocating money *as if* I had already hired them. Using this method, I was able to see if I had the cash flow to support that role. Even rainmakers don't necessarily produce sales in the first month. So for most businesses, I suggest that the FUTURE EMPLOYEE account have about six months of reserve in it before making the hire. That way, you not only know you can handle the monthly expenditure, you also have six months of reserve to handle that expense, in case it takes a bit longer to get that employee up to speed.

When eradicating debt is your primary focus, the owners may also need to cut their draw to make the business sustainable. That's a toughie for most of us. I mean, we have a life to live and deserve "a few perks." But it is that exact mentality of taking perks when the business can't afford it that keeps us in debt. Adjust the business (and your lifestyle) so that no new debt is incurred and that monies can accumulate to pay off past debt.

Then implement both a debt payment account and a profit account within your business. Allocate a predetermined percentage to both. The rule of thumb is, take 95 percent of the profit

---

*I strongly suggest that you work with a business coach. May I also suggest that your business coach be versed in the Fix This Next method to pinpoint your challenges? To find a certified Fix This Next coach, go to FixThisNext.com.

distribution that quarter to pay down debt, and keep 5 percent of it to reward yourself. Remember, you're a shareholder—to keep you positively engaged in your investment (your business), you must always get something.* That 5 percent will help scratch the "perk itch" for now. Realize that debt is a past expense that wasn't paid, so that payment of debt is really an expense. And the only way to pay off those debt expenses is by having more money available than you currently spend.

To pay down more than three hundred sixty thousand dollars in personal and business debt, I used Dave Ramsey's "debt snowball" debt eradication process. In a nutshell, he recommends maintaining all debt you have by making the minimum payments, and with every dollar left, pay down the smallest loan first, which allows you to remove it the fastest. While targeting higher interest rates first is logical, getting early and quick wins by focusing on small debt amounts builds confidence. Logically speaking, it may not be the best way to remove debt, but from the very human, behavioral aspect, the early wins of wiping out small debt builds a momentum that becomes unstoppable.

I went from being a not-even-close-to-a-badass angel investor to being a true badass debt crusher, and I loved every second of it. I got a thrill every time I paid down on what I owed—and that thrill was greater than anything I gained from spending money. This process is initially slow, but it must be consistent. You must build the debt-

---

*The priority of a business carrying debt is the eradication of that debt. But you must also reward the person(s) who have taken the risk of owning the business. So while paying down debt, a small portion of profits still goes to the shareholder. When all the debt is removed, then all the profits go to the shareholder. If you haven't yet read *Profit First*, the suggested target percentages are available for free at ProfitFirstBook.com.

crushing muscle. Don't stop until your debt is gone. I followed Dave Ramsey's system and the strategies I detailed in *Profit First* to wipe out all my debt within seven years. I paid off the small chunks at first, and bigger and bigger chunks as I grew my business. But every day I was chipping away debt. And every quarter, with my profit distributions, I was crushing debt and celebrating with 5 percent.

Today, I have zero debt, except for my mortgage. At the time I'm writing this, we're only two years into our new home, and I'm already working fast to wipe out that debt a decade before the thirty-year mortgage terms. Even though it makes logical sense to put more money into savings and investment accounts, the feeling of owning something free and clear makes your mind feel free and clear. When you have zero debt, you have achieved a big part of financial freedom. No worry about owing others anything—and that's a big motivator, comrade.

OMEN: Debt Eradication

Let's pretend that flipping houses has been your dream ever since you saw your first episode of *Fixer Upper* with Joanna and Chip Gaines on HGTV. There are tons of deals to be had out there; you just need seed money. The thing is, you don't have any money *left*. Your business is living off loans, and your FTN analysis identified your Vital Need is to eradicate debt.

Here's how you work the OMEN plan:

1. *Objective:* Debt isn't bad if it is driving profit. Debt is bad when you are beholden to it. You decide that over time you

will wipe out your loans and become your own bank. You will always have at least 20 percent of an average purchase price for a house in your area, in cash, in your bank. You can move decisively with this and won't have to hook or crook your way through purchases. Currently you have zero percent cash, and $100,000 of debt. To wipe out the debt you will use 5 percent of the top-line sale price. You sell houses on average for $300,000, which means $15,000 is going to debt each time. By your seventh flip you plan to have the debt eradicated. For now, it is hand to mouth . . . or, as you like to say, flip to flop. But that is about to change.

2. *Measurement:* You set up an account using the Profit First methodology and label it FLIP FUNDS. The average house you buy is $200,000 and repairs are usually $40,000, so you commit to having $48,000 or more in that account within twelve months.

3. *Evaluation:* Money is not a constant stream for you. It comes (and goes) in tidal waves. When you sell a house, money flows in. When you buy and renovate a house, money flows out. So you decide to set up a "debrief and evaluation" after every real estate transaction, which is about once every two or three months.

4. *Nurture:* While you have contractors, you are in the business alone, so you don't have a team to give you hands-on guidance as you build your cache of cash. However, you do put one hundred rocks, each with "$1,000" painted on it, on your conference table. After each flip, you take away the quantity of rock representing how much debt you have paid

down. Once all the rocks are gone, so is the burden of debt. Great visual! To address the "become your own bank" part, you set up a big poster board in your office with "20 percent" written on it, indicating the money you will immediately allocate from every sale to your FLIP FUNDS account. Under it, after every transaction you scratch down the current balance in the FLIP FUNDS account.

5. *Result:* Over the following year, you sold several properties and have allocated more than $200,000 into the FLIP FUNDS account. The next good deal that came through was for a $175,000 house that you could likely sell for $250,000 within four weeks. You had the cash to put down 20 percent. Shoot, you could even have put down 100 percent and still had $25,000 to do the repairs. More good deals will come, and you will be able to take advantage of them if they are a good fit for your company. The best part? No rocks in the conference room.

Need #2: Margin Health

Question: Do you have healthy profit margins within each of your offerings and do you continually seek ways to improve them?

Your clients want you to be profitable. I mean, they really, really want you to be accumulating wads of cash. Of course, they will never say to you, "Hey, I want you to squeeze every penny out of me," or "Please, please, please, rip me off." But what they *do* want is to be sure you'll be around for a while. They want you to back your offering, so that if they have a problem in two weeks, two years, or even two decades, you'll be there to solve it. They want you to serve them without distraction or worry about how you are going to survive tomorrow. They want your full attention. The only way to ensure your business will be there to support your clients and to have your head fully in the game is if you are perpetually profitable.

In my early days of entrepreneurship, I was always afraid to raise my prices. I believed, as so many business owners do, that if I raised prices, I would lose customers. Still, every time I sucked it up and raised prices to a level that I needed to sustain my company, I was blown away by how many customers stayed, and how many *better* customers then sought us out.

If you've read any of my previous books, you're familiar with the name Paul Scheiter and his company, Hedgehog Leatherworks, which creates and sells handcrafted knife sheaths. Paul is a very deliberate, conservative guy. When he takes a risk, he considers it so carefully and plans it out so thoughtfully that it ends up not being much of a risk at all. That is why when we first met I thought it odd that Paul sold his sheaths for $75. They were works of art. They also cost an easy $25 in materials and five hours of Paul's time, minimally. On a good day, that netted Paul $10 an hour—and that was before factoring in the costs of equipment purchases and repair, rent and utilities, part-time help, and incidentals. And yet Paul couldn't see that. He figured that he was making $50 for every sheath sold, because he was basing his costs on materials alone.

When I flew into St. Louis, Missouri, to meet with him and his company's board—who turned out to be his mom and stepdad—I gave him the cold, hard truth. "We need to do a four-times markup on raw materials and production time. We need to raise the price from $75 per sheath to $349." Four times is a typical markup from manufacturing to shelf space, especially for luxury items, if you want to be profitable.

Holy cannoli, if you could have seen the look on their faces—especially Paul's. He was terrified that increasing the prices by 400 percent would cause his loyal customers to revolt. Then I explained my logic. We had the $25 in materials cost. Then, we had the labor cost: $10 an hour to have someone do the work, times six hours (since a line worker likely couldn't achieve Paul's speed). That brought costs up to $85. Multiply costs by four and you get $340. Since consumers see $340, $341, $345, or $349 as basically the same, go with the higher dollar amount so that you can maximize profit.

"If you don't raise your price," I explained, "you will go out of business and have tons of debt. Most people won't even notice you raised your prices. Some will even say, 'What took you so long? And the customers who do get upset are looking for the cheap option. Do you really want customers who are the discount bin shoppers?"

Although he had serious trepidations, Paul followed my advice. Then, it happened: the first sheath purchase came in at $349, without complaint. No message asking, "Why did you raise the prices?" Nothing. In fact, from that day forward, demand for Hedgehog Leatherworks sheaths more than quadrupled. Apparently people had been judging the quality and value of Paul's product based on his price, and assumed his sheaths were of lesser quality. When they were priced at $75, they were just another commodity. When Paul charged what the sheath was *really worth*, people *saw its real worth* and bought more of them. This simple change put Hedgehog Leatherworks in a position of permanent profitability.

With Profit First Professionals, we have worked with more than eight hundred accountants and bookkeepers. In almost every case, we direct them to bump up the price for their services and they continue to get as many as or more clients than before. Not only do they now attract better prospects, their existing clients became better clients. You see, when a client invests more money in your offering, they become more vested in the outcome. The more they pay, the more they work on a successful outcome. I am not suggesting you ever rip off clients. What I am suggesting is that you bill what is fair for both your client and you.

OMEN: Margin Health

LED lightbulbs are the rage nowadays. For this example, you decided to jump into the hot business of cool lights as a retailer. Just one problem: the margins suck. After going through your Fix This Next analysis, you find the Vital Need sitting in the BHN. With the Vital Need nailed, it's OMEN time:

1. *Objective:* Inc rease profit margins on your LED lights so that you can support a 20 percent companywide *cash* profit. (A big jump from the current percentage, which is zero.) You generate about 17 percent gross profit per LED light sold, and the business is treading water.

2. *Measurement:* Calculations show that you should double your product margins so that you have 35 percent gross profit on each LED, instead of 17 percent. With that you can likely achieve a 20 percent bottom line for the company.

3. *Evaluation:* You have nice volume of sales activity, so the data is ideal for a weekly review. After your first week, you notice that most of your margin is in your specialty products, and that some of the standard stuff you sell is actually losing money. You keep up a weekly evaluation, and within a couple of months you can see that your greatest margins can be achieved through the sales of specialty products. You have enough sales volume to report this number daily.

4. *Nurture:* The team is totally on board with your profit-margin goal and created a display of specialty products at the front of the store in an effort to increase sales of those items. You start every team huddle with a number said out loud. You then pause a few seconds before the meeting continues. That number, everyone knows, is the average profit margin from the day before. For the last two months, it has been seventeen or eighteen every morning. But then, with the team's guidance, the first day comes when you say "twenty-three." The team goes wild!

5. *Result:* Your entire team reads *Why We Buy* by Paco Underhill, and with everyone's insights, you implement new strategies. Margins hit 31 percent just by changing the store layout. Next up is to start slowly removing some of the losing LEDs. You are confident you are going to blow by

the 35 percent gross profit. Your bottom line just surpassed 20 percent and you aren't done yet. The future looks extremely bright. I mean you *do* sell LED specialty lighting products, after all.

Need #3: Transaction Frequency

Question: Do your clients repeatedly buy from you over alternatives?

"I do everything for everybody."

"Whatever you need, we can do that for you."

"My niche is everyone."

Most entrepreneurs try to go both deep and broad with their offerings. They want to be all things for their hard-won clients and customers, and they see every "add-on" product or service as an opportunity to make more money. The problem is, you can't be masterful at all things because you can't allocate enough resources, or the best-suited resource, to all of your offerings. While it may be theoretically possible to streamline your complex business, that is a very costly process in both time and money. The most efficient solution is to reduce the number of offerings and to target a specific customer niche, since the more offerings delivered to a larger variety of customers results in an exponential demand on your resources.

In my books *The Pumpkin Plan* and *Clockwork*, I talk about finding your company's "sweet spot," that place where the needs of your ideal client meet your company's unique abilities *and* efficiencies. When you are laser focused on that sweet spot, you'll find that your time and money expenditures go way down. And bonus: your clients will be happier too.

Delivering a keynote about getting more customers at an NFDA event is downright strange. Why? Because NFDA stands for the National Funeral Directors Association. But there I stood, in Yankee Stadium (truly) in front of a group of funeral directors (seriously), and my job was to explain transaction frequency (I swear to you)—how to get the customer buying more often. I know, I know; when someone needs the services of a funeral director, it is kind of a one-time gig. And yet, even in the funeral industry there are multiple ways to increase transaction frequency. The first is to have the same customer buy repeatedly—which may work for you, but these funeral folks? Not so much. The second is to offer complimentary services and/or products without diluting your offering. And the third is to do both. For the funeral directors, we went with option two. Coffins, flowers, enhanced services are all options. Going further, one funeral home teamed up with a portrait painter to do painted memorials (and took a little piece of the action).

The lesson of transaction frequency is to seek ways to do more business more often with your clients, while never compromising or diluting the quality of work. In other words, ways to do more business with your clients while still knocking them dead. (Sorry, I had to say it.)

OMEN: Transaction Frequency

In this example, your landscape architect business has the Vital Need of transaction frequency. Customers love you and love your work. There is just one problem: plants live and grow without you. How do you get more work from customers without overly diversifying your offering (which can be the boar's path to a diluted business), while maintaining a reputation for excellence?

1. *Objective:* Increase annual transactions from existing customers by 50 percent. Currently, about 20 percent of your customers hire you back the following year to expand on your work. You want to increase that by 50 percent, so 30 percent of your customers buy from you the next year.

2. *Measurement:* You ask your bookkeeper to create a simple new report in your accounting system that shows how many customers are repeat buyers. It sums up the percentage of customers at the bottom of the report. You want to increase the number of repeat buyers by 50 percent within one year of today.

3. *Evaluation:* You determine that a monthly review of the report is a good rhythm.

4. *Nurture:* You set up a monthly pizza meeting with your team to brainstorm ideas. Someone suggests maintenance services, since so many clients don't do the watering and weeding themselves. The challenge with that fix is there is no margin in that type of work, plus tons of competition with landscapers, and it may start you down the boar's path of too much diversification. That is when someone on the team suggests that you set up a warranty program that will protect the homeowner if plants die or unpredictable weather tears up the landscape you designed.

5. *Result:* Some of the best margins in the world are in warranty programs. So you jump on it and it pays off! Almost 25 percent of new customers sign up for the annual warranty program you implement, with its automatic renewal. Your clients are paying you for the warranty year after year, increasing revenue and giving you opportunities to reconnect and share additional landscape design service ideas. You store a portion of the warranties in a WARRANTY SERVICE bank account you set up, and when a problem with a homeowner's landscaping happens, you have the cash available to honor the warranty. More important, you have even more cash available to honor the objective you had set for yourself. Well done.

Need #4: Profitable Leverage

Question: When debt is used, is it used to generate predictable, increased profitability?

Some businesses incur debt during a startup stage or a growth stage by expanding capacity before demand. While this is a common and effective way to grow, many businesses don't do adequate or proper projections on the time it will take to turn a profit on their investment. And even fewer set up "rip cords" to stop incurring debt or expansion if their projections don't pan out.

Debt can be a valuable tool when it is used to amplify clear profit opportunities. If there is a guarantee that taking on debt will result in more profit in a clearly defined time frame, you are positioned to leverage debt. Most businesses, though, don't leverage debt (while they may use that term); they are anchored by it. If debt is used to run the business operations, or to cover cost of goods sold, it is likely an indicator of a debt anchor.

Anthony Sicari Jr. is a business owner who knows how to leverage debt. His company, New York State Solar Farm (NYSSF), is the New York state licensee of SunPower, one of the most established providers of solar panels. As part of the deal, NYSSF buys in batches of at least eighty panels, which runs him about $75,000. On average, each home install requires about twenty-five panels, with some homes needing just fifteen and some as many as thirty-five. This means it takes NYSSF three to four installations to go through one of the SunPower batches.

Some companies would go into debt to cover the $75,000 cost up front. Not Anthony. He established terms with his supplier so that his company pays about $25,000 each week, rather than the full amount on receipt. This affords him time to take delivery on the panels, install them, and get paid in full for the installation, before the majority of the payment is due to his supplier. This simple negotiation put NYSSF on the cash-flow positive side, meaning they were able to get money in before it went out.

Anthony took it one step further . . . a very smart step further. He uses the Profit First method for his company, and so set up a bank account labeled INVENTORY. Every time he collects a payment from a client, a portion of that deposit goes into the INVENTORY account. Anthony then pays SunPower the $25,000 weekly payment out of that account. When we spoke, he had $40,000 in

this account, which meant he was fully ahead of the game. Even if ▼
he has a collections problem, he won't have a payment problem, ▼
which could eventually become a debt problem. And if a big order ▼
comes in and he needs a hundred panels, it's not a problem. ▼

Good debt leverage is when one dollar borrowed results in a ▼
predictable dollar-plus return, and quickly. In Anthony's case, the
lender is the supplier, and yes, he makes more than a dollar in return for every dollar borrowed.

OMEN: Profitable Leverage

For this example, let's say you sell silly signs for home decor on Etsy
.com. Top sellers are signs that say BUT FIRST, COFFEE; WAS TODAY
REALLY NECESSARY?; and your most popular, I'M OUTDOORSY. I DRINK
WINE ON MY PORCH. Signs are all about trends. When a new trend
hits, you have to be ready to jump on it. The Vital Need that you
identified is the ability to leverage debt for big profits:

1. *Objective:* To take advantage of new sign designs when you
   spot a new trend, or to create a sign that starts a trend. You
   know from past experience that the big expenditure is not
   creating signs; it's advertising. When a sign hits, you want
   funds to spend on Facebook. A $25,000 ad could easily bring
   in $500,000 in sales. The thing is, you need the $25,000.
2. *Measurement:* Before you drop big money on advertising,
   you ensure that there is an extremely high probability that
   every dollar you spend will grow your profit. You run a test

on a popular sign to see the results. First, you try a $100 spend on advertising and measure the results. Then, you try it with $500. Sure enough, advertising works, but the good profit margins are only on signs unique to you. That research gives you confidence, so you qualify for a revolving line of credit for $25,000 and sit and wait.

3. *Evaluation:* There is nothing to do for now except wait for the right opportunity to present itself, and when it does, to evaluate it daily.

4. *Nurture:* You put a sign over your desk that reads I NEED A SIGN THAT NO ONE ELSE HAS.

5. *Result:* Thank you, Mr. Snoop Dogg! While watching motivational content on YouTube, you listen to the speech Snoop Dogg gave when he received the Hollywood Star. In it he says, "Last but not least, I wanna thank me. I wanna thank me for believing in me. I wanna thank me for doing all this hard work." That's it! That's your great idea! You create the I WANNA THANK ME sign series for offices, gyms, homes. You run a test ad for a few hundred dollars and the sign sells out. Since the competition catches on fast, you have to move really quickly before they come up with a copy of your sign. That's when one of your employees gives a tweak to your evaluation: Don't measure results daily, measure them hourly. Time is of the essence. You use the OMEN parameters you set up, with the tweak of checking hourly, and do another ad test for $1,000. Gold! You get your best return on an ad spend ever. By the end of the day, you have manufacturing

ready and a contingency for back orders. You leverage the full $25,000 in debt. The sign moves faster than you can say Snoop Doggy Dogg, and the profits pour in.

Need #5: Cash Reserves

Question: Does the business have enough cash reserves to cover all expenses for three months or longer?

Desperate people do desperate things. That is *not* a position you want to be in. Cash will help you avoid it, and generally speaking, more cash will help you avoid it more. An adequate reserve of money enables you to navigate unforeseen circumstances with confidence. To allow business operations to continue unabated, or to take advantage of an unexpected opportunity, your business needs two to six times your average monthly revenue reserved in a VAULT account.

Here's how I was able to take advantage of an opportunity that came up. I had set up a VAULT account for Profit First Professionals and for my authorship endeavors. We had been casually looking for a bigger office space so we could expand, and we saw the value in owning property rather than continuing to rent. When a building in town came up for sale, we were ready and could pay cash for it. Cash reserves allow you to grab opportunities when your competition can't. Not to mention that cash in your business also increases its value.

When a potential buyer considers acquiring your business, the indisputable number one factor in your business's viability is how much cash it has made and held on to. Cash in the bank, generated from ongoing operations, is hard to dispute. With your VAULT reserved, your cash equity is up and your valuation is up.

Healthy cash reserves also brings a stability in decision making, allowing you to focus on the impactful issues instead of always rushing to the apparent issues. At the same time, since extra cash can soften the blow of mistakes and mismanagement, it may make it easier for poor decision making to continue. Because cash can be a double-edged sword, it should be reserved in a way that is not readily accessible to anyone (you, mainly), but is only available for risk mitigation and for exploiting opportunities. For example, you could require dual signatures for all checks and make that second person a trusted third party who is emotionally detached from the business. Or you could simply make it a pain in the ass to get the money out. Choose an independently run bank that is a long drive away and then disable online banking.

OMEN: Cash Reserves

Let's say you are in any business that comes to mind. This is a choose your own adventure. Remember those books? We'll simply call your business ABC Corp. You know the golden cash reserves rule, right? You need to have minimally three months of operating expense cash reserves—but you don't. Vital Need identified? Check! It is OMEN time.

1. *Objective:* Accumulate three months of operating expenses saved in cash reserves. You have a multimillion-dollar busi-

ness and you need $100,000 a month for operating expenses, which means you'll need $300,000 cash stored in a VAULT account.* You are doing pretty well, and have $150,000 currently saved, but need to double it.

2. *Measurement:* Your goal is to have $300,000 of cash sitting in the account within six months.

3. *Evaluation:* You will check progress on your VAULT balance every tenth and twenty-fifth of the month. You decide to allocate 5 percent of your INCOME (this is cash deposits) to the VAULT on these days—if you can afford it—allowing for at least one bad month out of six.

4. *Nurture:* You get your bookkeeper and accountant on board. The accountant agrees with the 5 percent and shows you a few ways to reduce your current operating spend and allocate the money to your VAULT. Your bookkeeper holds your feet to the fire and does the transfers.

5. *Result:* Things don't always go as planned. You didn't have one bad month; you had five. Customer demand changed unexpectedly. Good thing you started allocating 5 percent from the top line to your VAULT. This gave you a small additional buffer on top of the $150,000 you had already saved. But now you are pulling from the VAULT to cover other needs. Additionally, you are further cutting expenses and adjusting to a 2 percent VAULT contribution as you right-size your business. The VAULT account has given you

---

*I have a complete explanation of the VAULT account and other specialized accounts in *Profit First*.

the ability to have a soft landing for your business while your competitors are crashing left and right. You were a little lucky this go-around, and now you are acutely aware of the need to always have cash ready.

Fix This Next in Action

Remember Jacob Limmer from chapter 3? The owner of Cottonwood Coffee who discovered he had spent thirteen years in business and did not have a realistic idea of how much cash he needed to maintain his lifestyle—which is why he never cleared enough to support it.

Once you've fixed the right problem, you start the process again by reviewing the BHN from the bottom up. Since Jacob didn't have any other unchecked Core Needs in the SALES level now, he next evaluated the PROFIT level. Immediately, he realized he had an unresolved Vital Need: debt eradication. He told me, "When I think about our debt, I feel like the little Dutch boy trying to plug the dam with his finger." I think we all feel that way when we're drowning in debt. We wonder if anything will make a difference, because the problem seems too huge to conquer. (It's not.)

With the Vital Need pinpointed, Jacob implemented the Profit First principles and the debt freeze/snowball process. Jacob started killing debt. First, the small debts. Then bigger debts. Each paid-off debt bolstered his confidence and inspired him to push harder. Now wiping out his debt is an automatic process.

Jacob told me, "Before I paid it down, debt was a waterfall of small moral compromises. I would have to decide who I was going to pay on time, and which checks I would have to 'forget to sign' to buy myself a few extra days. I never wanted to be that guy, but I was."

Now Jacob pays every bill on time. "I have a sense of complete integrity again."

Jacob also offered insights about working through the Fix This Next analysis. "Prior to using the tool, I wanted to jump ahead. I constantly ignored the fundamental work. I lived in the land of delusion of another day another dollar. It took me going through this tool, and falling on the same spot [Vital Need] over and over again to admit, 'Okay, I must do this.' Also, it was a little bit of a bummer to realize and admit I am not in the LEGACY mode or IMPACT mode yet. But now I know that I'll get there, once I handle the fundamentals."

My favorite part of our conversation happened at the end of our call. Jacob said, "You know, Mike, I'm actually enjoying my business—for the first time."

Sweet, sweet words for this fella. I am getting emotional just writing this. I mean, why bother with business ownership if we are just going to be debt-ridden and depressed? You don't have to be riddled with debt, and you don't have to be anxious, stressed, or depressed. You simply have to focus on the fundamentals.

Chapter 5

ACHIEVE ORGANIZATIONAL ORDER

MY OLDEST SON, TYLER, IS A TRIVIA GURU. HE KNOWS A LOT ABOUT a lot and crushes the competition whenever anyone is foolish enough to play against him. (I stopped doing this when he was twelve. Now that he's an adult, I just make sure he's always on my team.) It was Tyler who told me an interesting fact about cancer. Did you know that our bodies are always experiencing the uncontrolled cellular growth that is technically cancer, and that our bodies keeps this growth in check? In other words, we don't "get cancer," we all already "have it"; it just becomes dangerous when our bodies can't control it anymore and it grows uncontrollably.

While writing this book, I mentioned the ORDER level to Tyler, and—warning, proud parent moment ahead—Tyler said, "It's the same with business. The problems are always there; it's just that we, like our body, are keeping them in control, *until* we are not."

Yep! That's my kid, showing off his head for biology and business, connecting the dots. Proud daddio right here. Excuse me while I wipe away the tear from the corner of my eye.

It's true. In business, there is always a natural tendency to move toward complexity. In an effort to respond to opportunities, to growth, and to changes in the marketplace, we routinely bring on more and do more. Maybe you're two steps ahead of the rest of us, but if you're like me and the entrepreneurs I know, you probably don't give much thought to the consequences of adding variability, beyond how it could serve customers and prospects. Though it may make sense at the time to expand our offerings, start a new project, or hire more staff, these changes can get out of control, which makes it impossible to create predictable outcomes. ORDER, a basic level in the entrepreneurial hierarchy, requires the improvement and dissemination of systems to achieve predictable outcomes. When you achieve this, the "cancer" that is unchecked growth and expansion is eliminated before it ever has a chance to get a foothold and stealthily kill your business.

One point I want to make clear—ORDER is not necessarily the *creation* of systems, though it can be. I'm not suggesting you spend months and thousands of dollars coming up with procedure and policy manuals. Though you may not realize it, you already have systems in place. Those systems may need to be improved upon, but they do exist. In many cases, they are simply the routines that you and your colleagues follow. Those are surely systems; they just need to be extracted from people's minds and stored in a repository accessible to others. For example, you can screen capture the process that one of your colleagues follows to do your company's invoicing—they do it out of habit, and the video screen capture now makes it a captured and preserved system.

One more important distinction I want to make is about *why* we improve systems. You may think, as I once did, that systems are all about getting more shit done faster. Nope. That's a vicious, exhausting cycle. When we achieve higher levels of productivity without organizational efficiency, we simply end up doing more work, not less. And much of that work is completely unnecessary, which means we are wasting resources.

When you bring ORDER to your business, you give it autonomy, because the company is no longer dependent on any one individual (including you). It has balance, strength, and fluidity. You are no longer carrying the business on your back, which means your company can continue without you—for a few days, or weeks, or years, or even a lifetime.

By the time this book goes to print, I will have already taken three four-week vacations in a fourteen-month period. Years ago, if you had told me that any business owner would take that much time off, let alone *me*, I would have told you that was absurd. Now I think business owners who *don't* take four-week vacations at least once a year are being absurd.

My first minisabbatical from the day-to-day operations of my business was from December 7 through January 7, and now I take that time off every year because it allows me to spend time with my kids when they're home from college and fully enjoy *and participate in* the holiday season. I learned so much during that break, and the business improved so radically, that I took another four-week vacation the following July. (Can you say Disneyland MaxPass? Good, I thought you could. So could my wallet.) Whenever I'm not on the road speaking,* I take weekends off. Shocker, I know. (Most entrepreneurs work weekends. But you already knew that, didn't you?) *And* I took a few shorter vacations. The lesson I finally—*finally*—learned? You are not a business owner if the business owns you. If you are needed for your business to operate, you simply have a job at a company in which you own a lot of stock. That's it.

The next time you go to a McDonald's, ask to speak with the owner. They won't be there. They aren't flipping burgers or frying fries. They are not in the glorified closet they call an office, and they are not working the cash register either. The owner is anywhere but there. Because every McDonald's relies on systems to run, not the owner's sweat.

You know those "Get Shit Done" mugs and T-shirts that entrepreneurs adorn themselves with? I want you to realize, as I have, that if you are getting shit done, it means what you are getting done is shit. Stop doing for your business, and start designing your business to run without you, permanently.

What did I do on my first four-week vacation? My wife, Krista, and I planned to travel to Quebec City (the most beautiful city in the Western hemisphere, in my opinion) and go on to visit family and friends in Europe. However, nature had a different plan. A few days before we were ready to leave, Krista broke a bone in her foot while out on a hike in the woods behind our house. The injury had

---

*I am blessed to have keynoted events ranging from entrepreneurial groups to franchises to associations to everything in between. I have a dedicated agency I work with, GoLeeward .com. They are great and accommodating. Check them out for your next speaker. I would be honored to throw my hat in the ring for consideration.

her in a boot for months, and the full recovery has taken about a year. Needless to say, broken foot = no travel. So we stayed home. You know what? It was awesome! I did projects around the house. We had guests over. We enjoyed sunsets and sunrises, watching from our hot tub (thanks to one of our quarterly Profit First distributions). I was able to help Krista recover—something I would not have had the time to do in years past. The entire vacation, I didn't check in with the office, not once.

That foot injury? That could have been me. What if I was the one knocked out of work for a few weeks, or a few months, or forever? The day will come when you and I won't be able to work in our businesses. The question is: will it be planned or unplanned? The only way to be ready for any eventuality is to give your business autonomy from you.

When I returned from my vacation in January, I met with my team to see how it went. In my absence they had stepped up into roles in ways they "couldn't" before my sabbatical, because I had been doing the work. Turns out, I was the one blocking them from stepping up. We also made an important discovery: we had a branding congruency issue. I hadn't realized how much I had been doing to ensure our messaging and branding was consistent until I wasn't there to do it. In my absence, the marketing became haphazard. Without me, marketing cancer appeared. So, a system for ensuring that our marketing aligned without me became my next one to create. After all this time off, it is so clear to me that my number one priority is to make myself irrelevant to my business. Once you nail SALES and PROFIT, your next mission is to make yourself operationally irrelevant through ORDER.

Need #1: Minimized Wasted Effort

Question: Do you have an ongoing and working model to reduce bottlenecks, slowdowns, and inefficiencies?

In his must-read book *Friction*, Roger Dooley explains how the taxi industry has not changed its prospecting system since 1950. It goes like this: taxi drivers trawl the streets for passengers while potential customers walk up and down city blocks searching for empty taxis. If you've ever tried to hail a cab in New York City, you know that means looking for a busy street, but not so busy that the traffic is at a standstill. Tricky business. When you finally get to a "good corner," you're competing with everyone else who needs a taxi. If it's near shift change for taxi drivers, you may be out of luck entirely, because they likely won't take any new fares. And if it's raining? Just forget about it. I hope you have a good umbrella, because you're going to have to walk . . . at least to the nearest subway station. This is a lot of wasted effort to get a ride! If you're a taxi driver, you spend your days driving around looking for passengers, or waiting outside hotels for passengers. When you do get a fare, you may end up driving that person to a part of town where no one else needs a taxi, so you have to drive back to a busy area to find another customer. More wasted effort. Dealing with confusing directions and handling cash and credit card machines at the end of the ride— more wasted effort. Or as Roger puts it, more friction.

Ride-sharing companies such as Uber and Lyft changed the game. They eliminated the tremendous amount of wasted effort. No need to hail a car. No need for the driver to go cruising around.

No worries about directions. No payment issues. It is all seamless. The customers and the drivers are happier, the process is smoother, and the profitability increases.

Many businesses become complacent about operations. We fall into a "this is just the way it is" mentality, not really giving much thought to processes. This is especially true for businesses that function within an industry that has set methods, such as the taxi industry. New drivers follow the same "systems" taxi drivers have always followed, even though time and effort are wasted every hour of every day. As my business partner Ron Saharyan at Profit First Professionals likes to say, "Grooves can become ruts."

Google had a person whose primary job was to ensure that the search page remained uncluttered. They were the guardian of the search page's unclutteredness, effectively. Departments wanted to add their functions to the coveted Google search page, such as mail or news functions. However, the goal of Google Search is fast, accurate results, and clutter slows down the navigation and brings unnecessary distraction. This person had to resist the entropy that businesses inevitably bring upon themselves. They had to remove any roadblocks or distractions that might prevent the user from finding pictures of Renaissance paintings featuring white peacocks, or whatever obscure thing they wanted to find, fast. When they launched, Google's main competitor was Yahoo!, a site where users contended with news, images, and tons of potential distractions. Because Google put a leader in place to fight wasted effort on behalf of their customers, Google won the search engine wars (for now). Not only did they win, but their company name became a verb that *describes* the act of searching for something on the internet. Way to dominate through efficiency and order!

Every business is a manufacturer, including yours. You may not manufacture things per se, but we are all creating an experience, a final feeling. And we all go through a sequence of steps to deliver that feeling. Look at the steps you take, see where there is a time pile (where things slow down and the time to complete a task piles up) or bottleneck (inventory or paperwork sits around waiting for someone or something to get to it), and clear it up.

While I describe this extensively in *Clockwork*, I want to add something I didn't mention in that book. We do need some degree of protective capacity. Meaning, you don't want to streamline and cut back on processes so much that when you have a sudden spike in demand it throws your business into a tailspin. (Remember, we are trying to prevent uncontrolled growth.) You need some excess capacity to cover the inevitable need to redo some work (ugh!) or to handle a surge of demand (yippee!).

Einstein is reported to have said, "Everything should be as simple as it can be, but not simpler." That is the goal of reducing wasted effort.

OMEN: Minimized Wasted Effort

In this example, let's say you own a computer company that installs and maintains computer networks at sporting arenas. You completed the Fix This Next analysis and it was clear that wasted effort needs to be minimized. The problem isn't with completing the

SALES stage successfully; your problems arise after the sale and installation. The new systems have a learning curve, and your customers tend to keep calling for months after an installation asking you to teach them a new bell or whistle. Time to OMEN this Vital Need, baby!

1. *Objective:* Reduce the amount of "after-the-install" training by 75 percent. Currently you have an average of 108 user calls coming into your office after an install. You intend to get that to 25 or less.

2. *Measurement:* Historically, you tracked the number of support calls and had to go through a mix of reports to determine the average number of such calls per client. Now you will track for each customer how many ATIs (that's the term you use for an after-the-install call) you do for them in real time.

3. *Evaluation:* You do one major install a month, and the support calls play out over another two months after it's complete. Since you are getting about three ATIs each day, you plan to track this on a daily basis. You will need roughly three months of accumulating data before you can make sense of your progress.

4. *Nurture:* You notify your tech and install teams on the new objective, measurement, and evaluation frequency. They confirm that the measurement and evaluation frequency make good sense. Then you ask them to suggest pathways to get there. Ideas spring up immediately, such as leaving a tech on site for the first week after an install to field questions, or video training, or simply "charging an extra fee every time

they call." One idea came way out of left field, but had both potential and a differentiator factor. What if during the downtime your client had during installations, their key staff came to your demo facility to learn the new system? The identical setups you rolled out were already in the demo office.

5. *Result:* You tried a mix of ideas, but the demo facility turned training facility ended up being the game changer. Installs went faster. Clients got work done (at your demo facility) and learned the system in real time, with your internal staff right there to help when they had questions. This also reduced distractions for your install team since clients were at *your* office during installs. When clients returned to their office, they were trained and ready to go. While some ATIs came in, it was now down to an average of 21 per client. Better than your target.

Need #2: Role Alignment

Question: Are people's roles and responsibilities matched to their talents?

Michael and Amy Port are the founders of Heroic Public Speaking (HPS). Their organization teaches aspiring and established speakers to become performers. From my experience, HPS is the best in the world at what they do—world-class teachers, teaching others how to be world class. I have trained with them myself and can tell you that everyone, including a guy like me, who has delivered more than five hundred keynotes, can greatly amplify their abilities using the HPS methods. Michael, Amy, and their team showed me how to make the shift from speaker to performer, and ever since I started implementing their techniques, I have received the greatest praise of my speaking career. For that, I am eternally grateful to them both.

Many people know about HPS, but few people realize that, in a mere eight years, Michael and Amy expanded their two-person training services conducted at public theaters and libraries to a group of elite instructors (and stellar support staff) at their own state-of-the-art performance facility in Lambertville, New Jersey.

How were they able to scale so fast while maintaining structural integrity? First, I know Michael and Amy shored up SALES, PROFIT, and ORDER, and that they are continually following their own tracking method to ensure they are on solid ground. Another aspect of their remarkable growth is their ability to align the right people with the right roles. Michael and Amy added new experts to their team and promoted those who were masters of their craft. They care as much about their staff's aspirations as they do their own. As a result, at every step along the way, their business leaped forward. They've even promoted former students—alums of their premier, comprehensive speaker development program, Heroic Public Speaking Graduate School (HPS GRAD). They developed a teaching fellowship program, moving students up to teaching roles and freeing up their own time.

That is what I am doing with Kelsey Ayres; I'll share her story later in this chapter. She is an amazing complement to the culture at our office, and my job is to actively find the roles that benefit the most from her raw talent. This is what HPS does, constantly. They find the right people, put them in the roles where there is a need, and (this is super important) actively seek to move that person into a better-suited role.

Role alignment is about putting the people in positions where they flourish, which allows the company to flourish. And in the roles that are left in need of people, to seek new people. It is not about putting people in roles where they don't fit and keeping them there. It's like doing a jigsaw puzzle. Your job is to match the piece to where it naturally fits; never jam it in.

OMEN: Role Alignment

In this example, you are a business book author. (I bet you're wondering where I got that idea.) You have built a following of readers and introduced products and services that support your books. Everything is hunky-dory, but you still have to take care of your next Vital Need. In this case, the Fix This Next analysis identified role alignment as the Vital Need. You have great people, but are not getting great results from them. Let's OMEN this bad boy, shall we?

1. *Objective:* Get your best people doing the right things, so they are happy and your company's efficiency increases. This goal is a little bit fuzzy, so to put some numbers around it, you run a blind survey with two questions. "How much do you love the company?" and "How much do you love your work?" The feedback is that people are rating love for the company a solid 10. Amazing! But love for their work is a scary low 6.

2. *Measurement:* You conclude that if your people do work that, for the most part, brings them joy, efficiency will be a natural side effect. So you set out to measure two things: 1. Love for the company, and 2. Love for the work. You intend to keep the love for the company at 10 and get love for work up to a 9. People can't always do what they love; there is always grunt work. But you can bump up the love factor from 6, for sure.

3. *Evaluation:* This is something that may take many months or even a year to play out, because you can't measure every day. The best approach is to make changes and then measure an immediate impact. Also, add a quarterly "How we doin'?" check-in.

4. *Nurture:* You meet with your team and tell them your plan to shift roles to increase their happiness. You ask each employee to list the top ten tasks they do that take most of their time. While your employees may be doing dozens and dozens of things, you know that the old 80/20 rule points to the fact that only a few things constitute the majority of their work. Next to each task they do, you ask them to provide a candid evaluation of love it, hate it, or meh. Then you ask them to write down five new tasks that they would like to do for the company that would bring them happiness. You get to work on the role alignment.

5. *Result:* You crushed it with this exercise. You found that some of your employees hated work that others loved and vice versa. You were able to easily shift work around and get most people doing work they love about 70 percent of the time. You also built a list of stuff that no one liked to do.

There were about eight things that needed to be done, not
necessarily bad work, just bad work for your current people.
So you ran a craigslist ad listing these eight things as the job
responsibility of a part-timer. Sure enough, you filled a position with a person who couldn't believe they found a job
doing exactly the work they love. Now you can get back to
writing those badass books you write, and you have a cool
story to share in your next book about role alignment.

Need #3: Outcome Delegation

*Question: Are the people closest to the problem empowered to re-
solve it?*

Here in the great U.S. of A., we have some beautiful university campuses, but the one that takes the cake—and you're going to be
shocked—isn't my beloved Virginia Tech. (Hokie, Hokie, Hi!) Nope.
It's Ole Miss, otherwise known as the University of Mississippi. As the
rising sun forms rainbow prisms on the freshly formed dew droplets
clinging to each emerald green blade of . . . blah, blah, blah. I'll stop
right there. You get the picture. The campus really is stunning. It
looks like the fairway of the eighteenth hole at your favorite golf
course. Perfectly manicured grounds. Birds chirping. You get the feeling that all is right with the world, and this campus is proof of that.

I'm not the only person who believes Ole Miss has one of the
most beautiful campuses in the country. They are known for it, and
it's not by accident. It's by design. Or better said, it's by ORDER.

In early 2000, Ole Miss realized that while other universities throughout the Southeastern Conference (SEC) were overloaded with new student applications, they had disproportionately fewer applicants. They knew they would benefit from more applications, which they assumed meant they needed to focus on sales. Sounds like a SALES level conversion Vital Need, right? It was, but to solve it, they ended up *also* fixing a Core Need on a different level: OR-DER. As I've said, you will occasionally find that resolving a Vital Need also addresses another Core Need or multiple Core Needs that are connected in some fashion to the Vital Need you are fixing next. Sounds like a riddle, doesn't it? Simply put, sometimes when you fix one thing you end up fixing another thing at the same time.

Now, they didn't have the trusty Fix This Next analysis to help them figure this out, so they went around the proverbial block a few times trying to fix it. Ole Miss researched how students select colleges, and the evidence was clear: a large number of students make their decision about whether to attend a school or not within the first few minutes of visiting the campus.

As they began to identify what would attract students to Ole Miss, they determined a beautiful campus would bring this benefit. Because no matter how many students they managed to get to campus for a visit, most would choose a different school based on a less-than-stellar first impression. At the time, they had the lowest-rated campus in the SEC, so they decided to go all out and beautify their campus. To accomplish that goal, they had to address the fact that their systems needed improvement. For example, at the time, it took their grounds crew ten days just to mow the grass.

Enter Jeff McManus, the head groundskeeper at Ole Miss, assigned to fix the problem. Instead of scheduling an executive meeting to brainstorm ideas, or Googling what other universities do, the first move he made was to call in the crew. Smart! Always gather the people who are closest to the problem and get their ideas for solutions.

The final analysis was that the campus wasn't in tip-top shape because the frontline people who beautify the grounds were being ignored. Jeff's first step was to elevate them. He gave them new uniforms and asked them for their ideas. As it turned out, the grounds crew knew exactly why the campus looked the way it did: it took forever to mow the one thousand acres, swallowing up the time necessary to beautify the place. The culprit behind the mass inefficiency? Low-hanging tree limbs.

The most efficient way to mow is in straight lines, and yet the crew frequently had to stop their riding lawn mower to move around a low-slung tree limb, or around another obstacle like a garbage can or squarely mulched area, all of which slowed them down. So the Ole Miss crew put a plan in place to ensure the trees on campus were trimmed at least ten feet off the ground, which gave clearance for the mowers and enhanced the look of the trees. The crew came up with other ideas, such as replacing the square mulch patches with round or oval mulch patches so they could easily mow around them, and moving garbage cans from the grass to paved areas along the sidewalk. Pine needles replaced wood-chip mulch, another beautification with benefits. Pine needles are natural, have a pleasant evergreen smell, and hold moisture better, reducing the need to water the plants as frequently, freeing up even more time.

With all the improvements made at the suggestion of the front line, the same crew was able to maintain the entire Ole Miss campus in half the time. This meant the campus could be maintained up to twice as frequently as before, keeping it in great shape at all times. And it also meant more time was available to work on other beautification projects.

Going through the BHN model, Ole Miss would have first considered if the two foundational levels below ORDER were solid. When I spoke with Jeff, I asked if they were sure their PROFIT level was shored up. The answer was yes. Ole Miss had a profitability structure in place. They just needed more students to leverage the profitable model they designed. However, the SALES level had a Vital Need. Working on the ORDER level, which is above the SALES level, would be a mistake, since the Vital Need was in SALES and you always work on the most impactful Core Need at the lowest level next. But sometimes you will be required to address another Core Need elsewhere in the BHN to fix the Vital Need. Sometimes the needs of your organization are simpatico.

As it turned out, fixing their prospecting issue in SALES *required* them to fix another issue in ORDER. That said, the primary goal was to address the Vital Need in SALES. In this case, by getting efficient at maintenance, they had a shot at killing two birds with one stone: Ole Miss transformed their campus and dramatically improved their number of applicants, posting eighteen consecutive years of increasing enrollment, thereby solving their Vital Need in SALES.

OMEN: Outcome Delegation

In this example you manufacture sunglasses. Your shop spits out about 1,000 glasses every day, and recently you've had problems with quality.

A lot of the glasses have scratches on them and are being rejected by your quality assurance team, which results in wasted materials and extra labor costs. Both are big no-nos for you. You have been banging your head trying to solve this outcome delegation problem yourself, but now are aware that the people closest to the problem are the most likely to know how to fix it. OMEN time!

1. *Objective:* To reduce the number of defective glasses from your current 100 out of 1,000 (a whopping 10 percent) down to 5 out of 1,000 (0.5 percent), which would surpass even what your best competitor achieves.
2. *Measurement:* You only need one metric for this, at least for now, and it is number of defective units per 1,000 manufactured.
3. *Evaluation:* Your shop produces a volume such that you can often see the impact of changes on the same day they are made. Since it takes less than twenty-five minutes for a set of glasses to go through the line, you can even see results in less than an hour. You want enough data to accumulate to achieve statistical significance, so you set the interval to a daily check. At 8:00 p.m. every night a report is generated, summarizing the results.
4. *Nurture:* You go to your team and tell them the problem. Then you ask the four people on the line along with the one person in quality assurance directly experiencing this problem to form a problem-solving committee. Their job is first to agree to the objective and measurement you have set, which they do. If they didn't, it would be their job to direct you on a better objective and measurement. Since they are all on board, you say, "You've got this, team. Fix this next!"

5. *Result:* A monitor on the shop floor displays three numbers: the total number of defects yesterday, a running total of the number of defects today, and the average daily defects for the last thirty days. They brainstorm improvements and run tests. After a few weeks, one of the line workers says that the metallic oxide pigments they are adding to the plastic is a new formula, and he heard from a buddy of his that they are highly susceptible to scratches. Going back to the old formula improves the defect rate, but it's not at target. Another line worker notices the lens grinder is making a nearly imperceptible noise on occasion, and concludes that it is slipping at this point, causing it to leave the scratch. The team immediately stops the line and inspects the inner mechanism of the grinder. Sure enough, some metal and glass dust has accumulated on the moving arm of the grinding wheel, causing it to make a small jump at times, which leaves a scratch. The obstruction is removed and defects immediately drop to only twenty per one thousand. A huge step forward. And the team is invigorated to figure out the next steps to getting down to five defects or fewer.

Need #4: Linchpin Redundancy

Question: Is your business designed to operate unabated when key employees are not available?

On June 6, 2019, I waved good-bye to my right arm and my entire brain. Her name is Kelsey Ayres. I call her my F.E.A.T.—Favorite

Employee of All Time. I can't even start to explain what an amazing colleague and friend Kelsey is to me. She joined my small business as a personal assistant in 2017, and in just two years positioned herself to run our entire organization. Kelsey is that smart, that driven, and that kind. She is beloved and respected by everyone at our office. And we had quickly become reliant on Kelsey.

By the start of 2019, Kelsey was still managing my personal travel itineraries (which are complex and always changing) and overseeing major projects, such as the rollout of our new email campaigns, our online sales, and my book launches. She also handled all our human resource tasks: hiring, firing, management, and payroll. And, she was the best damn podcast cohost on the planet.* Kelsey was doing all of that like a rock star, and that is when I realized I needed to let Kelsey go.

No, I didn't fire her. Hell, no! I will cling on to Kelsey with everything I can, for as long as she wants to work with us. Kelsey is amazing, but she had become a linchpin. If Kelsey got sick and couldn't work, or, God forbid, Kelsey wanted to take a vacation, the entire business came to a halt. Work would queue up waiting for her return. I would do a "quick check-in" with a "quick question" in a voice mail or text when she was gone, constantly demanding her time. I realized we had become fully dependent on her and that if we didn't have her around for any reason, the business was in serious trouble.

Earlier in this chapter, I shared the powerful strategy of the

---

*You can listen in right now by subscribing to my podcast *Entrepreneurship Elevated* on iTunes, Stitcher.com, or any popular podcast platform. Be sure to listen in to the sister shows: *Grow My Accounting Practice*, to get insights on growth strategies for accountants, bookkeepers, and other professional service businesses; and *Profit First Nation*, to get insights on growing your profits from others who have done it and insider tips from Profit First experts.

four-week vacation. I implore every owner to take a month off every year, if not more often. The goal is to get you away from doing the work and instead designing your business to do the work without you. The day you declare the four-week vacation, you will start looking at your business in a whole new way. Knowing the business can't depend on you will require you to make the business depend on itself. In fact, many entrepreneurs are so stuck in the doing that they don't take breaks or vacations for years (or decades). If you think that grinding it out will fix your business, and you have been grinding it out for years, you have proven that the grind will never work. Never ever.

With Kelsey, I realized that it isn't just the owner who needs to take a four-week vacation—every linchpin employee needs to do it. A business can't have critical dependency on any one person. We need redundancy throughout, because sheeyat happens.

I told Kelsey, "We need to let you go. Go and do something that you dream of in life. Take a sabbatical. You need to go so that we can build redundancy throughout our company for all the work you are doing. And so that you can elevate yourself from doing work to delegating work. And so that you can live life for its intended purpose, to do what brings you joy."

The day we declared her four-week vacation, which we subsequently made into an eight-week sabbatical, Kelsey's job transitioned from doing all the work she does to delegating the outcomes we wanted to achieve. Kelsey cross-trained Nina and Jenna on everything related to our finances. Kelsey got Paul and Jeremy up to speed on our marketing and online functions. Amber Vilhauer, founder of NGNG Enterprises, became our contractor for book launches (including this one). Liz Dobrinska of Innovative Images, who has been our graphic designer and web developer for more than ten years now, amped up our web technology and designed the *Fix This Next* book jacket. Jenna took over management of our email outreach and our drip campaigns. Newbie Lisa took over scheduling. Morgan became my go-to for speaking itineraries and travel. And Amy Cartelli stepped up in more ways than you can imagine, covering any other task at any time needed.

It took six months, but Kelsey had trained our team and recorded videos that captured every one of her routine tasks. By the week before she left for two months to travel through Asia and serve a struggling community, Kelsey had no work to do. Better said, she had elevated herself to a new job. She was managing our entire company, not doing the work for our entire company. The organization was stronger than ever. When Kelsey returned from the sabbatical, we made the announcement: Kelsey Ayers is the new president of our company. And I transitioned to being our full-time spokesperson.

Now we are working toward every key employee taking a four-week vacation annually. Do the same with your linchpins. Never be in the trap of dependency on individuals. You must have redundancy. It strengthens your business and gives a pathway for everyone to step up. That is the definition of a business that runs like clockwork. And a business that is performing at the highest level of ORDER.

OMEN: Linchpin Redundancy

Let's say you run a business directory of U.S. companies. Your clients buy prospect lists from you to do email blasts, traditional mailings, and call campaigns. You have a small team of curators who maintain the data to keep all the contact details as current as possible. It is a hard task, and when any of your curator team takes off or leaves, you feel immediate impact. Your Fix This Next analysis identified that you have the linchpin redundancy Vital Need. You are exclusively dependent on a handful of people to keep your data current, and even with all the advancements in technology, the accuracy of your data is still extremely dependent on these linchpins. You sell data accuracy, and your linchpins have you in a precarious position. You need to fix this next and build your OMEN scaffolding to do just that.

1. *Objective:* Free yourself of exclusive dependency on your curation team. They currently do over 80 percent of the data validation checks. It would be a miracle to get that down to under 10 percent, but your intention is just to cut it in half for now. If you can get dependency on your curators for validation down to 40 percent you will have a lot more breathing room.

2. *Measurement:* You track the number of updates you collect every day for new and existing businesses. Your curators track the number of updates they have confirmed. While the number of validations the curators do each day is of value, it is the number of updates that need to be validated by curators that matters. You want your curators to maintain their efficiency, and you want to reduce the demand on them.

3. *Evaluation:* Once you have a plan about what to do, you can track impact on a daily basis. As you strategize ideas you will generate interim goals.

4. *Nurture:* Your first job is to ensure your curation team that their jobs are protected and that they may serve different

roles in the organization as you make improvements. You tell the team the objective, measurement, and evaluation frequency. It is hard for people to break out of the "this is always how we did it" mentality, until one curator in the back says in a hushed tone: "Wikipedia." She goes on to explain that Wikipedia had this exact problem, and could not keep up with demand to update and maintain its entries. It looked as though Wikipedia was done until they opened up the system to be maintained by the end users: the public.

5. *Result:* You roll out this new idea of a public directory of all businesses. A Yellow Pages online, but Wikipedia-style. The directory will be totally free and totally maintained by the public. You incentivize businesses to keep their data accurate by giving them credits for updating and maintaining their data, by giving free ads on the site. Behind the scenes you have developed the most comprehensive and accurate database of all your competitors without the need for your curators to do all the work. You continue to sell the lists the way you always have; they are just better than ever before and your team can actually take vacations now.

Need #5: Mastery Reputation

Question: Are you known for being the best in your industry at what you do?

When it comes to a mastery reputation it is easy to think of the greats. What makes them great is their devotion to their craft. They do their one thing so well that people are compelled to buy from them and the fees for their services become less and less relevant.

When a client puts value in what you offer, they seek out the master. Here is the irony: when you have a mastery reputation, the customer will make extraordinary efforts to find you. For example, if my GP says he is moving to the other side of the country and is going to charge me five thousand dollars a visit instead of my twenty-five-dollar co-pay, and asks me to keep visiting him, I would laugh. I want convenience and affordability in a general practitioner. But if I have a specific heart ailment that has been addressed by a masterful heart surgeon on the other side of the country, and she charges five thousand dollars a visit, I will use her. I will find a way to get there, and I will find a way to get the money. It is all about getting this resolved the right way, by a master.

Generalists attract the general customer base and need to constantly learn diverse new surface-level skills to compete. The specialist attracts customers with specialized needs, and constantly improves their offering through deep learning and improvement.

I am not making a value judgment here. I am just pointing out that specialists have a much easier pathway to master their craft because they do fewer things more often. As a result, the specialist gets a higher-quality client for the most part. In the ORDER level, the goal for your business is to do fewer things better.

Stacey Duff is the president of a $28 million company, Pacific-Ocean Auto Parts Co. (PAPCO), which distributes General Motors parts in California and Oregon. She has figured out how to ensure that PAPCO is permanently profitable in a business structure that few could achieve. She has no control over her pricing.

GM sets the prices and tells her who she can sell to and who she can't. Stacey doesn't even have control over inventory costs. GM tells her what she must pay them. So how is PAPCO so profitable? They have a stellar reputation.

Stacey baked profit into every element of her business by ensuring that her team is the best in the business. Because she can't make a killing on a single product due to preset product margins, she makes it on running an efficient shop and delivering on time, as expected. In fact, Stacey is so good at what she does, GM often inquires how PAPCO does so well. Days before this book went to print, Stacey called me to share that PAPCO had been acquired. The new owner was captivated by PAPCO's reputation for excellence and took the ultimate shortcut to getting there by buying it.

OMEN: Mastery Reputation

Example time! Your restaurant is good, it really is, but you don't have a line out your door like the Mr. Sammy Soup next door. All he does is sell soup. You do everything! Wait a minute. Wait one stinkin' minute. Your Fix This Next analysis just pointed to the Vital Need of a mastery reputation. While you feel you are a master at everything, the fact that you don't have a line out the door every day definitely indicates your patrons don't see you as a master.

1. *Objective:* To have the reputation as the absolute best in your market. The key is to narrow down your offering and be better than anyone else at delivering it. Currently you have over twenty-five dishes on the menu. What if you narrowed

it down to just one? One thing, simply with variations. That is your big, slightly insane, objective.

2. *Measurement:* Revenue is an indicator. Food variety is an indicator. But the best is the line out the door. Can you be in a position where demand is constant, just like the Mr. Sammy Soup next door?

3. *Evaluation:* This is a gutsy one. You are going to make the change and then measure right after the change happens. You will give yourself the flexibility to go back to your prior business if your new test fails, and then test something else.

4. *Nurture:* You look through your sales data and see that you sell a surprising amount of Impossible Burgers. You are a comfort-foods type of restaurant with chicken nuggets and hamburgers and hot dogs, and you added the vegan Impossible Burger to your menu a year ago. You think your shot at mastery may be being the first vegan eatery in town and really nailing the flavor of plant-based alternative "meat" products. You run a test by opening a pop-up in your own restaurant for one month.

5. *Result:* You announce this new "temporary" restaurant while the other one "closes for vacation" for a month. Customers come and check out the new restaurant. You quickly learn new ways of preparing this product so it is tastier and juicer than any other plant-based burger. You improve at lightning speed, since you are only selling plant-based burgers, and the crowds increase. After a month you see the potential and decide to swap out your old generic restaurant setup with the new business mastery idea. It takes a year, and there are bumps and bruises. But with a rebranding and mastery of

these new burgers, you are the best in town—maybe the best in the world. Customers line up out the door. And I am happy to say that your lines are just a wee bit longer than your buddy Mr. Sammy Soup. Nice job, my plant-based burger buddy!

Fix This Next in Action

Stacey Seguin is a master level business coach at Tap the Potential LLC and draws on a broad swath of knowledge, certifications, and experience in helping her clients. I revealed the Fix This Next model to her one rainy morning at the company's retreat center in Alexandria, Louisiana. Ever since our meeting she starts off every coaching engagement with the FTN analysis and leverages it every time a client needs to identify their next challenge.

One of my favorite Fix This Next stories comes from Stacey's work with American Landscape and Lawn Science LLC. It is a company owned by Steve Bousquet, and in 2019 they were delivering their services to more than three thousand clients.

Only a few days after our rainy morning meetup, she was sitting in Steve's office in Franklin, Connecticut, using Fix This Next. They went through the simple process, starting at the SALES level and working their way up. They checked off everything that was stable, and confirmed that the thirty-six-year-old business had a strong foundation in SALES and PROFIT. However, when it came to the ORDER level, a glaring unchecked box lingered in front of them: linchpin redundancy.

Chris Bishop was managing the entire schedule for the company. Dispatch of service teams, management of clients' requests, and on-the-fly changes caused by unpredictable weather. A torrential rainstorm could have a ripple effect for weeks or even a month or more for some landscaping companies. This was not a problem for the puzzle master, Chris Bishop. Except for one aspect: the more he handled scheduling challenges, the less he communicated with clients, leaving people wondering what to expect. If Chris was out for a day, let alone on vacation for a week, the schedule was toast.

Steve and Stacey developed a plan. Get two employees backing Chris in scheduling and handling a good portion of the client communications so that the training was in the doing. They would watch Chris schedule and then communicate it to the clients. It was a great way to observe and learn the intricacies of scheduling, while actively addressing a weakness in communication.

Fast forward to May, the unofficial seasonal kickoff for the landscaping industry, and the linchpin redundancy was in place for the scheduling role. The prior year, the company fielded over seven hundred complaints specific to the communication around scheduling. As they approached the end of the 2019 summer season, complaints had dropped to under fifty. Chris Bishop was able to take his first two-week vacation ever. This business didn't miss a beat.

Chris is now stepping into a bigger role as COO of the company, and the company is stronger than ever, thanks to Stacey and thanks to redundancy.

Chapter 6

FIRST GET,
THEN GIVE

"I'LL TEACH YOU TO OWN A RESTAURANT FOR ONE HUNDRED THOU-sand dollars," Mark Tarbell said to the audience of entrepreneurs.

Mark is the owner of Tarbell's, one of the most highly awarded restaurants in Arizona. Along with Wolfgang Puck and Bobby Flay, he is one of the few winners of *Iron Chef*. And he has successfully run Tarbell's for more than twenty years. In other words, Mark is good. He is really good. So maybe he had a secret to owning a restaurant.

Sitting dead center two rows back, I was in my perfect "learning seat"—close enough to see the speaker perfectly, but not so close that I was looking up their nose. The other seats were filled with business leaders who had achieved massive success. To my immediate right sat Chris Kimberly (not his real name), the founder of one of the largest event-ticket brokers in the United States. I was not surprised when he leaned in extra close to listen to Mark. Chris had just bought five restaurants for, let's say, a little more than one hundred thousand dollars.

Mark said, "I hear it all the time, from the rich and the poor, from entrepreneurs to line workers: 'I would like to own a restaurant or bar someday. It would be my place,' they tell me. 'I can be there whenever I want. I can make friends. I can have my table.' The reality is a restaurant is just like any other business.

"I have seen restaurant after restaurant crash, because they don't understand that you have to build the business from the ground up," Mark continued. "You need to attract the right customers with your unique offering. You need to ensure your profit margins are on point and you need to master the manufacturing process of creating food for the masses. You need to manage a highly perishable inventory and a highly transient staff. And you have to do all of that efficiently. *And*, even if you accomplish that, you have about a five percent chance of making it. The competition is extraordinarily fierce."

I knew that stat was pretty much on the mark. According to CNBC, nearly 80 percent of restaurants close before their fifth anniversary, and 60 percent close within the first year. The truth is, most new businesses go belly-up in the first few years, and regardless of the unique details of each closure, the reason they fail boils down to the same thing: they didn't focus on stabilizing their foundation.

Mark continued. "If you are looking to own a restaurant because you think it will be cool, or want a place that your friends love to go, or for any other reason besides mastering the process by devoting your life to it, I suggest you use the hundred-thousand-dollar method of buying a restaurant. Here's how it works: Find your favorite restaurant, the one you want to own. Go there twice a week for dinner or lunch, and get your favorite meal and wine. Make sure to tip your waiter a hundred dollars. Tip the chef a hundred dollars. Tip the bartender a hundred dollars. Tip the owner a hundred dollars. And tip the valet a hundred dollars. Do this every time, twice a week for a year. By the end of that year, you will own the restaurant. You could call at seven p.m. on Valentine's Day and say, 'I want the best table in the house,' and, trust me, it will be there waiting for you. You will own the place."

The audience laughed. Well, most of them. Chris with the five new restaurants didn't laugh, and neither did the other restaurant owners. They took copious notes on what they needed to fix next, as in immediately, in their business. I also took notes about Mark's story, so that I would always remember that wanting to own something and wanting to grow a business are two very different pursuits.

Many of us come to a point on our entrepreneurial journey when we think, "Holy crap! I've been kidding myself about the health of my business." It's that moment when we wonder if we wanted to own something or if we wanted to grow a business. When we question our choices. When we acknowledge and accept that we have been pushing through, working long hours, and putting out fires in the hopes that the next big deal would solve all of the problems. Often, that moment comes after we see all that we need to do to shore up our business. You may be experiencing this right now.

After completing your Fix This Next analysis and reviewing the descriptions and sample scenarios of the Vital Needs in SALES, PROFIT, and ORDER, you may be having your own "Holy crap" moment, realizing that you have a lot of shoring up to do. Take heart. That you have come to this moment is a sign that you are on the right track.

Accepting reality is a necessary, albeit somewhat painful, step in growing a truly healthy business. Now that you have faced what needs to be done, you can go forth and fulfill your entrepreneurial destiny. You have the insight you need to build a foundation so strong, nearly any dream you can dream is possible.

I know you're not in business because you want to look cool, or because you have grandiose ideas about owning a business, as Mark Tarbell suggested some restaurateurs can be. You're a weirdo like me: You actually *like* owning a business. You're not playing pretend here. You're all in. So mastering the process of running your business, as Mark noted—that's something you are willing to do. That's something you want to do. You want to be great at this, and you want to see your business rise, and grow, and get stronger every day. Now you know how to do that.

The vision for your company is usually the strongest the day *before* you open the doors. That is the last day your dream is still a dream. The next day it is all about execution, and it is that very next day when the challenges and opportunities, issues and solutions, pour in.

It is in this day-to-day management of our business that we lose sight of the dream. Not that the dream is no longer important, it just doesn't matter as much at the moment as getting through the day. But for most entrepreneurs I know, this day-to-day survival

becomes the new norm. The dream still exists—it just gets put on
the back burner for now, in the closet later, and stored away in the
cobwebbed attic soon after that.

You had that dream for a reason, my friend. You wanted to have
a better life. Or provide your family with a better life. You saw an
opportunity to do work that brings you joy. Or you saw an opportunity to control your own destiny. Or, I suspect, you wanted to have
all the above and more. The good news, regardless of where you
feel you are in your entrepreneurial journey right now, is that you
are closer to your dream than you think.

The "Get" and "Give" Levels of the BHN

Now we've come to the "musical bridge" part of this book, a short
chapter in which I am asking you to take a moment and consider
what it truly takes to make an impact on the world and leave a
lasting legacy. Just like in your favorite song, the bridge is the connecting piece between the front and back of the melody. With
SALES, PROFIT, and ORDER, you have heard the front end. Now
we are going to transition to the last stages. But you need to hear
this bridge first . . .

The best cup of coffee I ever had was in Guatemala City. Philip
Wilson, founder of Ecofiltro, was giving me a tour of the area,
showing me the beautiful architecture and the renowned restaurants, when we stopped into a little place to drink "the world's best
coffee." Sure enough, it was.

Phil is an energetic person. As he showed me the improvements
being made to the city, he radiated joy. He wasn't always that guy,

though. No, he was a very different guy. A guy who sat in front of the TV staring at CNBC, watching stocks. That was before he learned that 80 percent of families in Guatemala do not have clean water.

As Phil explained, to purify their water, people were boiling it, which required them to burn at least three logs a day. The cost was fifteen to twenty dollars a month to boil the water, and most families could not afford that. Phil's sister had started a nonprofit to help solve the problem, but she couldn't raise enough money to reach her goals. Phil realized that the scope of the problem could not be fixed with donations, and it surely couldn't be resolved by focusing on IMPACT alone.

So Phil made Ecofiltro into a social enterprise in which urban sales of water filters finance the distribution of filters to rural areas at an affordable price. Ecofiltro has one superclear objective: to get clean water to one million Guatemalan families in rural areas by the year 2020. I am excited to report that, as I write this in 2019, they are on the verge of achieving their goal.

Sadly, so many noble efforts are launched without a plan of sustainability. These businesses want to change the world, but don't consider a sustainable source of cash flow, internal financial health, or efficiencies. I can't tell you how many for-profit businesses I have observed that qualify as a not-for-profit, and that's certainly not what their founders intended.

They are all for doing great impactful things but ignore the foundation of the BHN, something that all businesses, for-profits and real not-for-profits must follow. Businesses that ignore the "get" foundation of the BHN (SALES, PROFIT, and ORDER) and focus on "give" (IMPACT and LEGACY) first are destined for perpetual struggle at best, or a quick demise, most likely. Even a not-for-profit business needs to have a foundation of health; they are businesses too.

Phil followed the BHN compass to a T, though he would have called it "good business practices." To make an impact on the water-quality issue in Guatemala, Ecofiltro would first have to shore up the three foundational levels of a business's needs: SALES, PROFIT, and ORDER. Sales and profit fuel the good work they do, and ensuring ORDER is in place allows them to amplify it to meet a world-changing goal.

As we parted ways, I asked him about the quality of his life today. Phil took his final sip of coffee and said, "I always thought business was about accumulating money. I thought that one day in the distant future, I might become a philanthropist. At that point I would stop trying to get money and start giving money. But Ecofiltro taught me a new truth: business is about both the getting and the giving, in synchronicity. You must establish a business where you facilitate growing demand, where you are profitable, and where you are efficient. You must continue to get all these things to be able to give."

No longer focusing on accumulating more money, Phil's life and work are now rooted in impact, and he's still accumulating money at the same pace. Funny how that works, huh?

"I can't even explain the amount of joy this business brings me," he added. "I think I will be doing this for the rest of my life."

You were put on this planet to have impact, there is no doubt in my mind, and that impact is not achieved by sacrificing yourself or your business. This is not a martyrdom game. You must nail the foundation of SALES, PROFIT, and ORDER so that you can then give back to the world through IMPACT.

Getting and giving plays like this on the BHN:

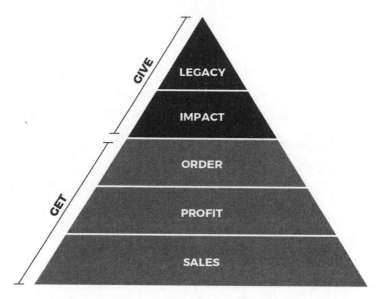

Figure 6. The Get and Give Levels of the BHN

To be able to give in a sustainable way, you must first focus on getting your foundational BHN levels in order. I know I'll get push-back from some business leaders about this, especially those entre-preneurs who subscribe to the give-first approach that some experts tout. Maybe you're shaking your head right now too. Let me be clear, I'm not suggesting that generosity as a guiding value is mis-placed, nor am I suggesting that giving back is not important. I want you to give back. I want you to give back so much and so hard that you can see a measurable improvement in our world. I *want* you to make the world a better place. I just want you to have a solid foundation from which to do that important work.

As a reminder, here's how to use the BHN as your checklist to figure out which Core Need is your Vital Need that you must fix next:

STEP 1—Identify: Within each level, check off the Core Needs that your company is adequately meeting to support the level above it. If you aren't adequately meeting a need or don't know, leave it unchecked.

STEP 2—Pinpoint: Evaluate the lowest level that has unchecked Core Needs. So if you have unchecked needs in PROFIT, IMPACT, and LEGACY, work at the lowest level of the three: PROFIT. Of the needs you left unchecked at that level, which one is most crucial at the moment? Circle this as your Vital Need.

STEP 3—Fulfill: Generate measurable solutions for the circled Vital Need. Implement your solutions until the Vital Need is adequately addressed.

STEP 4—Repeat: With the Vital Need fixed, find the next Vital Need by repeating the three steps above. Use this process for the life of your business to navigate through challenges, maximize opportunities, and continually uplevel your business.

Thomas Edison said, "I always invented to obtain money to go on inventing." Perhaps your way of giving back is to continue to innovate and create offerings that make our lives easier or better. I would argue that if you are solely focused on creation (another form of giving), eventually your business will collapse under the weight of your ideas. Why? Because you didn't shore up the first three levels of getting.

Comparison Versus Contribution

Two magnetic forces drive the get and give parts of the BHN. I saw it in Phil's story, I have seen it in mine, and I see it in every entrepreneur I meet. Either their primary driver is their ego's focus on comparison or the primary driver is their superego's focus on contribution. People who are focused on keeping up with the Entrepre-Joneses constantly revert to the base of the BHN. Then they must sell more, because they need more money coming in to show significance through size. They need more profit to collect more trophies, more things, more stuff. They need a business that can do more automatically, so they can do more in other businesses. This is not necessarily bad; it fuels the economy and it serves employees. To be clear, I am not saying people driven by ego and one-upmanship is wrong. I know very good people who are in this position. What I am saying is that I found it to be empty. It's not fulfilling.

Smiles 4 Keeps, a pediatric dental clinic in Bartonsville, Pennsylvania, is one of those businesses (or at least *was* one of those businesses). They got so stuck in the get phase that as a result some would say they ended up losing their integrity. In 2018, Smiles 4 Keeps sent out letters to the parents who were late scheduling routine dental visits, informing them that if they did not make a dental appointment for their child, Smiles 4 Keeps would report them to state authorities for "dental neglect." In other words, for child abuse. The letter they sent to "neglectful" parents who had not scheduled a timely dental visit concluded, "To keep your child as healthy as possible and avoid a report to state authorities, please call Smiles 4 Keeps immediately to schedule a treatment appointment within the next thirty days." This caused an uproar among parents and made the news. They ultimately rephrased their letter so that it was nonthreatening, but the damage was done. They may have scared parents into appointments and created more sales, but at what cost? It looks like Smiles 4 Keeps is actively trying to change their reputation, but the 2018 reviews linger. A simple Google search of "Smiles 4 Keeps Neglect" produces pages and pages of not so flattering news.

It's important to check yourself so that you don't get stuck in get-only mode. Many companies never make it out of the first three levels, and that's a shame, because entrepreneurs have the power to solve all of the world's problems. I really believe that. But without this understanding of getting to give, occasionally a business slants so much to the get-only part that it becomes cancerous.

The call for contribution is not perfect either. Some people just want to give and give, and do it through self-sacrifice. They are flogging themselves. They confuse the feeling of sacrifice with success. I know people like this (you do too), and they are good people—but they are focusing on the wrong part of the pyramid at the wrong time. They are "giving 'til it hurts," and that hurt puts them right out of business.

If you feel compelled to help certain clients because they need you in the worst way but can't afford you, you are on the verge of sacrificial giving. And if you continue to service them, even though the lack of money is slowly putting you out of business, you are an all-out sacrificial giver. Generous, but not sustainable, for sure.

When you go out of business from your unsustainable giving, countless other potential clients will never get a chance to experience you. The self-sacrifice of giving until it hurts ends up hurting the countless clients who will never benefit from what you offer, because your business got wiped off the map.

With our musical bridge over, let's get back to our core melody, shall we? On to the IMPACT level of the BHN!

Chapter 7

EVOLVE FROM TRANSACTION TO TRANSFORMATION WITH IMPACT

A FEW MONTHS AFTER MY FIRST BOOK, *THE TOILET PAPER ENTRE-preneur** came out, I was sitting at the kitchen table with Krista. I had received an email earlier that day from an entrepreneur and I'd printed it out to show her. The entrepreneur shared how he had applied one of the strategies from that book and saw immediate results.

Krista read the email twice. First, she skimmed it. Then she re-read it slowly, deliberately, absorbing each word. When she had finished reading it, she looked me straight in my eyes, and after a long pause, said: "This is what you are meant to do, Mike."

The entrepreneur's journey is a jarring ride with extreme highs and lowly lows. I knew that my new life as an author had left both of us feeling uncertain about how it might affect our future. In fact,

---

*I wrote *The Toilet Paper Entrepreneur* to give startup businesses a big leg up over the competition. You can check out the book at ToiletPaperEntrepreneur.com.

after I lost all our wealth, lost our home, and failed to healthfully manage my (self-diagnosed) functional depression, things were a "wee bit" strained for Krista and me. It was as if we were in a junker car racing down a twisted road, with Krista in the passenger seat with no seat belt, and me in the driver's seat, but with a broken steering wheel and missing brakes. Scary for the business owner, raw terror for the business owner's spouse.

So hearing a vote of confidence from my wife in that moment meant everything to me. Knowing she supported my career as an author touched my soul.

But the ride kept on rolling (and careening) on, and four years later, Krista and I sat at the exact same table in our kitchen, probably over the exact same meal, facing the reality that for most of us, authorship—any entrepreneurial journey, really—is a very slow climb.

This time, Krista said, "You need to get a job, Mike."

This time, her words felt like a *stab* to my soul. Getting a job is the ultimate gut punch to any business owner. It is the undeniable admission of complete failure. That the entrepreneurial journey is over. Stick a fork in me, I'm done!

Krista was right. She was right about authorship being my calling, but also that we needed money badly. By this time I had published a second book, *The Pumpkin Plan*, and affirmations from readers came in daily. But the money did not. Our financial situation was barely improving.

I had started my first business at the tender age of twenty-three, had built and sold two multimillion-dollar companies, and for the first time in nearly twenty years, found myself searching the job listings for work. I would soon discover that "entrepreneur" is the worst credential to have on your résumé, maybe second only to "author." No one wants to hire an entrepreneur (and a serial entrepreneur has it even worse), because they know that we are not meant to be employees. It's pretty likely that we will leave the job in pursuit of another business idea.

So, for better or worse, I doubled down on my mission in life to eradicate entrepreneurial poverty, and to do it via authorship. At the same time, I had to acknowledge that being an author *was* my business. I had been expecting lightning in a bottle: the overnight bestseller. I needed to take what I knew about growing a company and apply it to authorship. I couldn't focus on the goal of changing the world until I shored up my basic needs: SALES, PROFIT, and later, ORDER.

No way was I going to get a job. (I can feel your fist bump, mi entre-amigo. I know you get it.) And no way was I going to compromise my family anymore with a pipe dream. That night I realized that before I can serve the world, I need to serve myself. Before I followed my instinct to be all about IMPACT, I had to align my instincts with the foundational truths of business and get my sales, profits, and efficiencies in place, in that order.

Today, I'm proud to say that the crazy ride seems to be not so terrifying anymore. We are coasting along at a consistently high level (for now)—no crazy loops or terrifying drops. Krista's words, *This is what you were meant to do*, were, in fact, prophetic. She was right. This is what I was meant to do. The reason I am still here, still pulling for us business owners, still seeking solutions to make the entrepreneurial experience simpler for *you* so that *you* can do what *you* were meant to do, is because I put raw instinct aside, followed the BHN compass, and took care of business. I created other revenue streams related to my books, and ensured that those revenue streams were shored up. The impact you want to make is important, but you can't pull it off until you have all of the base levels humming. No one can. I sure as heck couldn't.

I shared my story with you because I want you to always remember that you can't skip ahead. When you fix a problem, go back to the base and work your way up the hierarchy. Every. Single. Time.

If your three foundational levels are in good shape, you can focus on IMPACT. At the IMPACT level your offering is no longer just transactional; it's transformational. People see the greater good your organization delivers—both in their own world, and for the world at large. With all of your five basic needs at the IMPACT level satisfied, price is a secondary consideration for your clients. They are no longer asking, "Is this the best deal?" Instead, they are asking, "How can I be part of this?" Their consideration becomes more about the movement or meaning than merely consumption. At the IMPACT level, you build brand loyalists, ambassadors, and lifelong members, *because your company is on a mission for a greater good.*

Let me be clear that every business and every offering must have an impact on your ideal clients in order to be consumed by them. The distinction is that at this level of the hierarchy, stewardship is the priority. This is where the win is *everyone* winning—you, your clients, your team, your vendors, your industry, your community, your country, and our world. Yes, I know that's one of those Big Beautiful Audacious Noble Goals (Big BANG) that seems like fantasy, with outcomes that may seem hard to measure. Eliminating entrepreneurial poverty is also a big goal, but I am determined to keep at it until every business owner lifts themselves from all the unnecessary struggle so that they can follow their mission. And because this is what I am meant to do, I'll keep at it until my final breath on this planet. That's a promise.

The IMPACT level is about living into your Big BANG. I want to be clear that this is your choice. This is all about you and what lands with you. It does not need to serve the entire world and it does not need to be life changing, as defined by other people. This is your definition and you are completely within your rights to change it.

I remember meeting with an entrepreneur who had lost his spouse to a horrible disease. He looked at me with tears in his eyes, and with noticeable discomfort said, "Mike, my life's purpose is clear. I need to put food on the table for my children every day, and do it by myself. I am sorry I don't have a Big BANG. But this is what I need to do."

I started to cry (I am a major co-crier), and said, "That *is* your Big BANG, my brother. That is a massive purpose for your life, and that is an absolutely noble IMPACT to make with your business. I can't think of anything greater for you."

Two years later I met with him again, and he shared again with tears. "My Big BANG was to feed my children, and my business has done that. I have expanded it now and we are feeding other children with single parents. I found the ultimate connection time for families is over dinner. If single parents have a warm meal ready so they don't have to worry about cooking, they can focus on time with family, and that changes the world I have experienced." Spot on, brother! IMPACT is about changing your world, by your definition. It's not about the size of the community you're serving; it's about the size of gratitude you feel as you give the gift.

In this chapter, we will address the five Core Needs you must fulfill in order to ensure that you are making the IMPACT you set out to make.

Need #1: Transformation Orientation

Question: Does your business benefit clients through a transformation, beyond the transaction?

Cooking serves quite a few souls, and in different ways. The Lost Kitchen in Freedom, Maine, has eight tables and one seating per night. This means they can serve about forty-five customers—for dinner. That's it. No second or third locations. No breakfast, no lunch, and no Sunday brunch. No happy hour. No line out the door trying to get a table. Oh, and they are only open nine months out of the year. Only eight tables and one seating, and the Lost Kitchen is a remarkable, if not magical, success. In fact, despite their remote location, theirs is one of the hardest reservations to get in the country.

After losing her diner and her home in a divorce, chef and owner Erin French opened her farm-to-table restaurant with the intention of providing more than a meal for her customers, whom she considers guests. She wanted to create a dinner-party experi-

ence in keeping with the pace, values, and ideals of her community. And she wanted a restaurant that freed her from the typical
grind most chefs endured without question.

Shortly after opening the Lost Kitchen, they received international acclaim. French received three coveted James Beard nomi-
nations (like the Oscars for chefs) and published her first book, *The
Lost Kitchen: Recipes and a Good Life Found in Freedom, Maine*, in
2017. By then, managing reservations had become overwhelming
for her and her staff of fifteen women. Their voice mail was always
full, and people showed up in person with gifts to try to bribe their
way into a reservation. One week, they received more than ten
thousand phone calls.

French wanted a solution to the problem that would not tax her
staff and would be in keeping with the experience of dining at the
Lost Kitchen. She came up with the idea of opening reservations
for only ten days during one month of the year. Specifically, from
April 1 to April 10. Just one small catch: the only way to make a
reservation request is via a three-by-five-inch postcard.

In their 2018 season, they received more than twenty thousand
postcards. Those who were lucky enough to be chosen from the
bins of cards received a phone call confirming their reservation.
The postcards have become part of the experience for the staff as
well. Before each dinner, they line up the cards from that evening's
guests, so the preparations are personal, and that feeling continues
throughout the evening. For many diners, the Lost Kitchen is a
transformational experience that shows them how dining out *can
be*—beautiful in its simplicity.

When we focus on the transformation we want to provide for our clients rather than on the transaction (making a sale), we are truly making an impact on their lives.

OMEN: Transformation Orientation

Let's say you run a business called the Best Bean. You sell ground coffee to local stores and directly through your website. People love your coffee, but you want more for your people. You want to transform their lives. Here's your OMEN:

1. *Objective:* Move your customers from just drinking a good cup of coffee to that coffee launching a great day. You really want customers to feel transformed and inspired every time they have your coffee.

2. *Measurement:* Unsolicited reviews will work best here. You get great online reviews for the taste of your coffee, but that's pretty much it. What if people start posting reviews saying that your coffee changed their lives? That is what you will measure.

3. *Evaluation:* If necessary, you will nurture some strategies and modify the measurements as your progress. Reviews currently trickle in at a rate of about one a week. So for now, you will evaluate the data monthly.

4. *Nurture:* You and your Lean Mean Grinding Bean (the title for your COO) come up with a plan. You will use a simple spreadsheet to track review date, the rating, and the topic (taste or transformation). You come up with a plan to

achieve your objective: blend Snapple caps with Chinese restaurants. You will include "cup messages" with every bag of coffee you sell. Since each bag makes about fifty cups, you include fifty individual messages in a simple dispenser included in the bag. When your customer opens a new bag of coffee, the dispenser is on top with the simple instruction "Read one with each cup." Messages such as "As beautiful as coffee is, you are far more beautiful." And "Good moments come from a good cup of coffee and a good person. You have both right now."

5. *Result:* Your COO comes to you during the nurture phase with measurement tweaks. There is an unexpected review source: Instagram. People are posting their Fortune Coffee on Instagram daily. So you add Instagram shares to your spreadsheet as another thing to track. The online reviews also pile up as your coffee affirmations get people thinking about themselves and their possibilities for the day. Maybe you aren't saving lives, but you are inspiring them. Transformation well done.

Need #2: Mission Motivation

Question: Are all employees (including leadership) motivated more by delivering on the mission than by their individual roles?

If I say, "Remember hell week?" most business owners can recall a grueling stretch when it was "all hands on deck"—everyone working round the clock to get a job done. But the worst hell week for my business cannot come close to comparing with what the Navy SEALs call Hell Week. After weeks of training in which they are torn down physically, the candidates endure six days of massive sleep deprivation and constant physical and mental harassment. Hell Week is designed to make them quit, because when the SEALs are in combat, the SEALs *cannot* quit, or the mission will fail. If they can survive Hell Week, then they move on to the next "buildup" phase of training. Most don't—only 25 percent of candidates make it through.

During Hell Week, one of the six days is spent in the Tijuana Sloughs, where the mud is so deep it can swallow you up. In his 2014 commencement address at the University of Texas at Austin, Navy SEAL admiral William H. McRaven told the story of how he and his fellow candidates survived this phase of Hell Week. First, they paddle down to the mud flats. Then they spend the next fifteen hours submerged in the mud, up to their heads. The weather makes it worse—they have to deal with freezing temps and wind. Perhaps the hardest part is dealing with the constant pressure from their instructors to quit. On this day, they told the men they could all leave the mud if five men left.

With eight hours to go, McRaven noticed that some candidates were about to give up. He could hear their chattering teeth, between the murmured groans. In his speech, he recounted what happened next.

"And then, one voice began to echo through the night. One voice raised in song. The song was terribly out of tune, but sung with great enthusiasm. One voice became two, and two became three, and before long, everyone in the class was singing. The instructors threatened us with more time in the mud if we kept up the singing, but the singing persisted. And somehow, the mud seemed a little warmer, and the wind a little tamer, and the dawn not so far away."

It was the singing that reminded Admiral McRaven and his fellow candidates *why* they could not quit. They motivated each other to stay the course and complete the mission. The following morning, 100 percent of them had survived Hell Week. Admiral McRaven served as a SEAL for thirty-seven years, though his title changed as he moved up the ranks. He served in several wars, including the Persian Gulf War, the Iraq War, and the War in Afghanistan. Most notably, he organized and oversaw the execution of Operation Neptune Spear, the special ops raid that led to the death of Osama bin Laden.

Now, you may be thinking that business isn't as serious as combat. It's not life or death. For most of us, that's certainly true. And it's also true that without a "song" to cling to and help you get through tough times, or busy times, or even to just *do a better job*, you and your staff may want to quit. Quitting can be literal, as in leaving the company, or it can be that slow slide toward ambivalence and complacency that makes it nearly impossible to grow a business. If you want your team to help you make an impact on the world, you need to give them something to believe in—a song to sing. That song is your company's mission.

Once you realize your mission is your song, you and the people who choose to work with you will be able to quickly pick out the melodies that move them. The repeating tune of "our mission is to increase shareholder value" that so many businesses default to lands like an out-of-tune, drunk guy belting out "Free Bird" at the local dive bar. We all have heard the lyrics a million times before, and this guy singing it surely ain't no Lynyrd Skynyrd. Good words, that motivate no one. However, missions such as that of Make-A-Wish—making wishes come true for children with life-threatening medical conditions—or Tesla—prioritizing the environment by creating industry-leading products that overtake less environmentally directed products—do resonate with many people. Your mission is your melody. Identify one that connects with your soul and start singing.

OMEN: Mission Motivation

Your hypothetical company makes plastic pack rings. You offer a large variety, which is a convenience for your customers, and you don't see them going away soon. However, the rings have a negative impact on the environment. They end up dumped in the ocean and sea life gets caught in them. Pictures of sea turtles stuck in pack rings and drowning are all over the internet. It is time someone makes it their mission to fix this and your heart calls out to step up and be that someone.

1. *Objective:* Define your mission as a provider of convenience that doesn't do so at the cost of our environment. You want everyone on board, from your C-suite to your design team, working on creating a more sustainable alternative to plastic pack rings.

2. *Measurement:* You know it is successful if your sales go up and your pollution goes down. What if you made the gutsy call of having a distinct color coding on your pack rings, so

people can instantly identify your new environmentally friendly product? This way everyone knows they are yours, and if you succeed with your mission it is highly visible. Of course, if you fail it is highly visible too.

3. *Evaluation:* This is something that can take years to roll out, but the innovative thinking can start today. So you will first measure the frequency of ideas generated to achieve this objective. Once you are in production, you will measure the sales of your new designs and the impact.

4. *Nurture:* The classic way to get the team in sync with an objective is scoreboards and spreadsheets. You want to go big on this, though, so you make one very public statement. In the main reception area of your building you install a massive saltwater fish tank. Then you take the team on a special sea turtle tour at the local zoo. The team embraces your objective. For the first time in their lives, their mission isn't to make more money or spit out more product. It is to offer something that everyone wants without hurting our fellow inhabitants of planet Earth. The ideas abound and the team is all on board for being "the someone" who takes a stance.

5. *Result:* Your company innovates a biodegradable six-pack ring made from corn husks and a secret mixture of other biodegradable ingredients. The new pack rings are notably more expensive than plastic, but you will get costs down. One team member gave you a better idea than a unique color. She suggests a unique logo. With that idea in hand, you emboss an image of a sea turtle on each pack ring, and become famous for it. Customers demand the "turtle-friendly

six-pack" guys. Your business grows consistently and your mission is unstoppable. Over the years you become one of the biggest contributors supporting sea-life rehabilitation.

Need #3: Dream Alignment

Question: Are people's individual dreams aligned with the path of the business's grand vision?

Amy Cartelli is a critical member of my authorship team. She was hired to manage orders, and during Kelsey's sabbatical, she stepped up to do blogs, handle customer inquiries, and to pull miracles out of hats. She works part time, and she applied for the job because she wanted to get a little social time and light work to break up the quiet parts of her day.

Amy told me right up front, "I want to be there for my family." That was her goal. Her husband was often on the road for work, her oldest son was in college, and she spent a lot of time caring for her aging parents. Getting all of her family together at the same time was not easy, and opportunities to spend time with them could come up at the last minute. Amy was already living her dream: to be with her family and be the matriarch she enjoyed being. Our goal was to align her job with that dream.

So we created a job for Amy that, if she were to drop it for a week, could be picked up the following week or by someone else. We set it up so that she can literally call out sick from work while she was actually *at* work. As a result, Amy loves working with us and we *looooooove* her. When she's in the office, she is 100 percent focused on delivering outcomes. And when someone else needs coverage, she steps up without ever being asked. Amy has stayed with us for years—through her father's passing, and through her own battle with cancer.

As you may recall, Kelsey went on an eight-week sabbatical. Her dream is to be of service to people who are in need of help and hope. Before that, though, her dream was to buy property in the woods. So we went to work on her first dream and structured a four-day work week, which allowed her to have a full-time job with us and a three-day weekend to work another job. She used the pay from her second job to save for her house. Dream fulfilled.

The lesson is this: to fulfill your employees' dreams, you don't need to come up with cash constantly. There are countless innovative, cost-effective ways to help your colleagues' dreams come true. First, you have to find out what their dreams are.

Author C. B. Lee writes young-adult fantasy and sci-fi novels. She also writes the *Ben 10* comic book, which, if you are a ten-year-old, makes her a rock star. C.B. also has a full-time job, and she took the job in part because her boss was supportive of her author career. She was able to take time off work to promote her books at Comic-Con and at book conventions. She works her ass off for her boss, and he allows—scratch that, encourages—her to continue to pursue her dreams. I know you are not surprised. Of course she does anything for the boss, because the boss does anything for C.B. That's how we humans work.

When your employee's job is designed to align with their personal goals and dreams, they will perform better for you and they will stick around. This is because you are making an impact on

their lives that goes beyond a paycheck and health insurance. You
are helping them create the lifestyle they want to live and become
the person they want to be. You are putting them first, and as a result they put you first. For an excellent book on the topic, pick up
The Dream Manager by Matthew Kelly.

OMEN: Dream Alignment

In this hypothetical, you have the most popular ice-cream shop in
town, The Dairy King.* People love the variety of flavors and the
amazing creaminess that "only the king" can make. The thing is,
your staff is just there for the job. Yes, they are proud to work for the
king. And they are shockingly reliable for a food-service business.
Still, when you ran the Fix This Next analysis, it became clear that
you don't have dream alignment.

1. *Objective:* To have the business serve your employees as well
   as it serves your customers. Employees are happy, but their
   jobs are more a means of income for themselves than anything else.
2. *Measurement:* This one is pretty simple. Do your employees
   see The Dairy King as a place to work or a place where their
   dreams come true? A simple anonymous survey confirms the
   obvious: it is just a job. A good job, but still just a job.

---

*This is a hypothetical name for this story, and everything I write about The Dairy King is
made up. But I do want you to know that there is a very real Dairy King ice-cream shop on
Long Beach Island in New Jersey. It is my favorite place to go. So next time you are visiting
Jersey in the summer, swing by Dairy King one night. Chances are I will be there. Let's get
some soft serve. I'm buying!

3. *Evaluation:* This is something that will play out over time. You will hold quarterly meetings with employees and record their progress on their dreams. Then you will do surveys two times a year to see if The Dairy King is becoming a creator of dreams.

4. *Nurture:* You designate your longtime employee, who has been with you for twelve years, the dream manager and follow the protocol in Matthew Kelly's book, *The Dream Manager.*

5. *Result:* This one takes time to play out—a few years, in fact. Some employees love your objective from the start; others are confused by it. You stick with it, and The Dairy King gets a reputation for making personal dreams a reality. After a few years, you no longer need to run ads for employees; people want to come here because it is the ultimate launchpad for life. Jobs at your company are hard to come by because people don't want to leave. The best part is that in your community it is now seen as an honor to work for The Dairy King . . . where "ice dreams" really come true.

Need #4: Feedback Integrity

Question: Are your people, clients, and community empowered to give both critical and complimentary feedback?

Have you ever seen those notices in some public bathrooms? No, not the "For a good time call Mike's mom" hurtful graffiti. I'm talking about that small sign right next to the exit that reads: "How is our facility?" or "How clean is the restroom?" Below the question you'll often see three buttons. One is a green smiley face, one is a yellow neutral face, and the last one is a red angry face. That system is a powerful, timely feedback system, because with the simple press of a button the janitorial crew knows if the bathroom is in need of maintenance or not, and can send someone to clean up messes right away.

In the past, the janitorial crew would have to check the bathroom during their regular rounds. However, if in between those checks a bathroom got messy, or a sink overflowed, or the local high school football team just came through after eating Taco Bell, the next people to use the space were in for an unpleasant experience. A bathroom could go unattended for a long time and upset many a customer. With the simple green, yellow, and red feedback system connected to wi-fi, the bathrooms are monitored by the users. A regular stream of green pushes, with an occasional yellow or red push, means things are a-okay; you can't please everyone. When there is a disproportionate volume of yellow or red pushes, a janitor is immediately dispatched. That is how you leverage the feedback loop.

As I shared earlier, my life's mission is to eradicate entrepreneurial poverty. (You can hear me beating the drum here, right?) My path to achieving that is through delivering real, highly actionable solutions for business owners through my books and speeches. It's not enough, though, to put our offerings out in the world and pray. To ensure we are making an impact, we need to hear from the people. We need to hear from our clients, our vendors, our community. We need to hear from our team. Are we delivering on our purpose? Are we staying true to our mission? Are we making an impact on their world? Our world?

I set up a feedback loop for my business to ensure that I *am* delivering on my purpose. In each of my books, I invite readers to contact me. Each request is tailored to the promise of that book. I get letters and calls from readers every day, and I get emails every hour. And let me tell you, when I read just one of those emails, any stress I might be feeling seems to melt away.

The powerful thing about this form of feedback is that it is timely, direct, and gives me the chance to respond. I daresay that 99.99 percent of the emails are rooted in kindness, but it does not mean that each one is a compliment. Some people have told me that my book *Surge* kinda sucked. Not that it was a badly written book or concept per se, but that I deviated from my strengths. Instead of providing a tool that made entrepreneurship simple, I went into entrepreneurial theory. Important stuff, but not my strength and my readers felt comfortable enough to tell me the truth.

As a result of that feedback, all my books since then have been and will be only about providing a tool that simplifies an aspect of entrepreneurship, just as I hope I am doing with *Fix This Next*. In the superrare case, I get a nastigram, such as, "You dress like an idiot and write like a moron. Those cheesy vests are ugly and your horrible 'jokes' in your books are even uglier." I ignore those and keep wearing my cheesy vests and dropping my cheesy joke bombs.

I am only getting the rare red or yellow button pushes, and that's more than okay; that's expected. It is when I get a disproportionate number of red and yellow button pushes that I need to take notice, inquire, and adjust. But at least for now, I get a pretty constant stream of green button pushes. I love hearing how one of my books has served someone in a small way or big way, and that affirms that I am on track.

If possible, I suggest you set up a feedback loop that is consistent with your "love language." If you haven't read the international bestseller by Gary Chapman, *The Five Love Languages: How to Express Heartfelt Commitment to Your Mate* (read it!), the basic premise is that there are five primary expressions of love, and each of us responds better to one of them. They are words of affirmation, acts of service, receiving gifts, quality time, and physical touch. Shocker of shockers, my love language is words of affirmation. I know this about myself, so I set up my feedback loop not only to measure impact, but to allow me to feel loved by my readers. Look, it may sound self-serving, but it's actually fuel. Fuel to keep going. Fuel to keep improving my offerings. Fuel to fulfill my mission. Fuel to serve my life's purpose.

OMEN: Feedback Integrity

In this scenario, you run a boutique hotel in a popular tourist area. Competition is fierce, but your hotel is known for its attention to details and its unparalleled cleanliness. The question is, are you sure your customers feel that way? Doing your Fix This Next analysis identified feedback integrity as your Vital Need.

1. *Objective:* Establish a system where you receive integral feedback from clients on the cleanliness and tidiness of your hotel. Even though you are known for this, you want to raise your game and so set a "never a pillow out of place" goal.

2. *Measurement:* Rather than getting reviews after a guest checks out, you want real-time reporting. You decide to model your measurement on the green, yellow, and red systems in some public bathrooms, which allow patrons to update staff about the state of the bathroom by pushing a green (clean), yellow (needs cleaning soon), or red (this bathroom is gross!) button. I wonder where you learned about that bathroom system? Anyway, your system will be simpler—just green or red. Either your facility is impeccable or it's not.

3. *Evaluation:* For you, this is a real-time system. Hour by hour, minute by minute, your hotel must be on its game.

4. *Nurture:* Your hotel manager is already doing checks on all these areas and, you might add, is doing a great job. You need more checks completed faster, yet hiring a new person is not in the cards. That is when your manager suggests that you set up a red/green app. Every guest gets a free app, and if they notice anything that doesn't thrill them, they push the red button and the concierge texts them in order to take immediate action. However, your guests don't complain much, because the experience is so good. It is the "meh" moments you need to catch. You decide to use a version of a secret shopper: people who are willing to walk your hotel for about two hours and do fixes on the spot—such as picking up the loose hair on the ground and trashing it, or noticing a squeak in a door and immediately telling maintenance about it—earn credits toward a free night's stay, or a few free drinks at the bar. After they put in a hundred hours, their name is added to the "Guardians" plaque on the wall.

5. *Result:* Locals, notably the ones who are neat freaks, keep your hotel pristine. Your reputation for excellence is noted in reviews, but it always has been. Now you see it from repeated guests and in media features.

Need #5: Complementary Network

Question: Does your business seek to collaborate with vendors (including competitors) who serve the same customer base in order to improve the customer experience?

I'm a thrifty guy in most regards. I generally avoid coffee shops because I can make my own cheap coffee, thank you very much. Still, a local shop won me over and earned my business. When I walked into Boonton Coffee Co., a very thin guy with an even thinner Vincent Price mustache greeted me. (If you don't know who Vincent Price is, you've never seen a great horror movie.)

I ordered a chai tea, and he said, "I suggest the place down the road. Their tea is awesome!" He went on to explain why their competition's tea was the best, and how to get there. And then he added, "But please feel welcome here. Come back with the tea and stay here. Or if you like, I can make you something else. We just don't have chai tea."

I settled for a coffee. Mustache guy made it, and then said, "That's on us, since it isn't what you wanted." Wow! That's when I realized that Boonton Coffee Co. isn't in the business of selling coffee. They sell comfort. So it doesn't matter to them if I go down the

street to "the other place" to get a chai tea. They know that I'll
be back to get my coffee from them. Now, I know what you are
thinking: why don't they just start offering chai tea? They could, of
course, but that would be their first step to compromising the OR-
DER stage of the BHN. To be masterful at anything, you must focus
on your one thing. Their one thing is coffee, not tea. I suspect they
know the day Boonton Coffee Co. becomes Boonton Coffee & Chai
Tea Co. is the day they start their march along the dangerous boar
path of a generalist. They know you will always have the greatest
impact when giving the customer exactly what they need—even if
it's from a competitor. Or in the case of Santa Claus, *especially* because it's from a competitor.

Remember the movie *Miracle on 34th Street?* If not, add it to
your "must-watch list" along with the Vincent Price horror movies.
This Christmas classic is the one where Santa Claus (as in the *real*
Santa Claus) gets a job as a Macy's store Santa. Most people focus
on the plot of the story, in which he has to prove he's the real Santa
to stay out of the loony bin, but there's a particular scene that is the
standout for me. Part of the job of a Macy's store Santa was to in-
form parents where they could find the toys their children asked for
in the Macy's store, except the *real* Santa didn't follow protocol.
Instead, if Macy's biggest competitor, Gimbels, had better-quality
roller skates, or a cheaper red wagon, he would tell parents to buy
them over at the other store.

At first, the Macy's store manager was livid. All those potential
customers walking out the door! And then, word got out that
Macy's was trying to transform their customers' holiday shopping

stress by giving at least a modicum of relief with better deals. Suddenly, Macy's was flooded with customers. Sales skyrocketed, and the line to see Santa went out the door.

Sure, that's just a movie, but you'd be surprised how it plays out the same way in real life. Whether it's my local coffee shop, or Progressive Insurance allowing you to compare rates at other companies to see if you can get a better deal, embracing your competitors and other complementary vendors builds trust with your customers. When you are looking to have the greatest impact on your customers with or without you, the client's appreciation for you will skyrocket. What are some ways you can collaborate with other organizations who serve your base?

Before you write this one off as one of those "it only happens in the movies" examples, let me remind you that Amazon embraced their competition in a big way. Rather than try to outprice vendors, they decided to partner with them. Now nearly anyone can have an eCommerce presence on Amazon. Even when a customer chooses a vendor on an Amazon affiliate site over Amazon itself, they win. Amazon gets a percentage of sales, and they are seen as the go-to online store for everything from dental floss to tiny houses. (Oh, and I hear they still sell books.) Besides that, Amazon also serves as a fulfillment center for some vendors, which means Amazon makes even more money on fulfillment fees than they would if they stocked the same products themselves. So when you see "Fulfillment by Amazon," that means they are making out like bandits.

OMEN: Complementary Network

Let's pretend you're a special-event florist. You sell different floral arrangements for weddings, birthday parties, and other celebrations. Your FTN analysis points to the Vital Need of a complementary network. Time to OMEN this bad boy.

1. *Objective:* You want to have the ultimate impact on your clients by being devoted to their celebration as much as they are. Yes, you will always provide spectacular flowers, but more importantly, you want to ensure that their celebration is the greatest it can be, even if it does not include your services.

2. *Measurement:* As you dig deeper into the IMPACT and LEGACY levels, you find that it is harder to get quantitative data and it is more about qualitative data, such as goodwill and brand reputation. That doesn't make it less important by any stretch of the imagination, it just makes it more difficult to track. You decide to rely on customer feedback and online reviews, because that is where you expect to get the most direct feedback. Yes, sales should increase over time too. But for now it is simply trying to gauge how customers feel.

3. *Evaluation:* You provide flowers for about three celebrations a week. As such, the reviews don't come in frequently. You measure them monthly, but don't see much traction there. So you decide that it may be better to measure the size of your network of complementary vendors, and then start a follow-up campaign with your customers to see how the

referrals went. This shift in measurements serves you and you can see the traction you are having.

4. *Nurture:* The online reviews end up being a strong indicator of your progress. You see comments such as "This florist went above and beyond any vendor I have ever worked with," and your favorite, "My florist had more contacts and helped me more than my wedding planner. Unbelievable!" You also have a follow-up plan in place to talk with your clients to learn which vendors didn't work out. Sure enough, some introductions you made were bummers. You cut those vendors from your list, and keep building your network on a simple premise: your company will only work with other vendors who care about the celebration as much as the customer.

5. *Results:* Your reputation for being of service precedes you. You have a remarkable network of specialists, including one company that creates specialty chandeliers for events. That is all they do, and they specialize in megacelebrations. They have made you their top referred florist.

Fix This Next in Action

The ultimate privilege I experience as a business author is to watch the trajectory of a reader's entrepreneurial journey over the years. For me, the journey of Jesse Cole and his team has been top banana for me. His team takes all the bananas in the bunch . . . the Savannah Bananas.

I first heard of the all-star league baseball team when the owner,

Jesse, contacted me. He had read the first edition of *Profit First*, implemented it in their business, and because of his commitment to the profit process and to doing what others in the industry don't do, the Savannah Bananas have experienced unheard-of success. They have sold out the entire season for 2017, 2018, 2019, and all indications are that 2020 is sold out and tracking to be their best fiscal year ever.

I have been to multiple games, and had the honor of throwing out the opening pitch during one of their games in 2018. In true Savannah Banana wacky style, the baseball was swapped for toilet paper (Jesse's homage to my first book, *The Toilet Paper Entrepreneur*) seconds before I walked out to the pitcher's mound. The dozens of hours of pitching practice did *not* pay off.

Jesse and I have become friends. We have broken bread together, enjoyed many a long conversation, and Krista and I have even spent a weekend at his home on Tybee Island, Georgia. Jesse has also become a willing guinea pig for any new entrepreneurial tools I develop. So it is no surprise he was one of the first business owners I approached with the Fix This Next analysis.

To set the stage (cough . . . baseball field), in 2019 the Savannah Bananas baseball team surpassed $3.5 million in revenue, had twelve full-time employees, and one hundred fifty part-time employees. They lead the league in attendance, revenue, profit, and countless other categories.

Jesse went through the analysis and was able to check off all the needs at the SALES, PROFIT, and ORDER levels. As he went through IMPACT, he triple-checked the transformation orientation need. There is no question that he was delivering baseball games; he was giving families clean, no-screen fun time. They are truly transforming families and peoples' lives.

As Jesse finished running through the IMPACT level, there was one box he couldn't check: complementary network. He had made progress in that area, but it was incomplete. So Jesse got to work. First, he defined the outcome he wanted, and he looked at one great success he had already achieved in this category: beer.

Jesse is in this business for the long term. He wants to extend the brand and grow it outside the confines of the stadium. If he squeezes people in with a shoehorn, maybe he could somehow expand attendance from four thousand to five thousand people. Jesse knew his ability to impact people in the stadium was maxed out, but if he could extend the brand outside the confines of the stadium, he could transform far more lives. He figured out the pathway to do this was through complementary vendors.

Jesse had struck a deal in the prior year with the Service Brewing Co. in Savannah, Georgia, to brew the Savannah Banana Beer with no royalties. The brewing company did not need to pay for the logo or name, they just had to make and can the banana-flavored suds and sell them at the games. The brews flew off the shelves. Service Brewing Co. had an instant hit on their hands, and the baseball team had another way people were experiencing the Savannah Banana culture.

That's when it hit him . . . or better said, that is when it opened his eyes to what was right in front of him: TV exposure.

Because of the Savannah Bananas' uniqueness, a regular stream of TV programs showcased the team. ESPN continued to feature them more than any other minor-league or all-star team. Jesse said,

"I realized we could leverage not just a complementary network, but a literal network."

With his Vital Need pinpointed, Jesse didn't need to pick up a phone and cold-call. He looked through all the past requests that had come in and vetted them. In the stack of media inquiries there was a note from a company called Imagine Entertainment.

Jesse returned the call as the baseball season was coming to a close. For the final two games of the 2019 season, Jono Matt, a producer from Imagine Entertainment, was sitting in the stands and taking it all in. He wrote up a pitch for a sitcom. If you have ever seen *Arrested Development*, think that, but with baseball.

Of the forty-five hundred different pitches that have come to Imagine Entertainment, twenty have been selected for further development. And only one of them had a unanimous vote as the number one top choice to develop. Yep, you guessed it . . . the Savannah Bananas.

The story will play out while this book goes to print, so you and I will see on the other side whether the show materializes. That said, it has a real shot. It has a real shot of changing millions of lives. And it has a real shot, because the owners of Imagine Entertainment are Brian Grazer and Ron Howard. The gents who created *Arrested Development*, and some of the greatest movies and TV shows of modern time.

The Savannah Bananas are on the brink of radically extending their impact, because Jesse pinpointed his company's Vital Need and concentrated his energy there. Wouldn't you know it, when something comes into focus, sometimes you find out it has been sitting in front of you the whole time.

Chapter 8

SPARK YOUR COMPANY'S FOREVER LEGACY

IT WASN'T JUST A CANNONBALL; IT WAS AN ENTIRE LOST CITY. IN Kansas of all places! (This will come full circle in just a moment.)

When I first started using the BHN for myself, I was confident in the three basic levels (SALES, PROFIT, and ORDER), but something didn't feel complete. My heart told me something was missing.

Many businesses elect to continue to work these three levels into perpetuity. In fact, a longtime friend of mine (who will go nameless, to protect the guilty) has built a business that has more than just sustainable sales—it has grown year in and year out for more than twenty years now. It is wildly profitable. The business runs, if I may, just like clockwork. He only goes to work "to do something with my time."

I asked him what his plan was, and he said, "I think I am going to fully retire in the next few years, when I turn fifty."

Then what?

"I'm going to golf pretty much every day. Probably twice a day."

I am not trying to be a judgy-judge again, but my spidey sense tells me that my friend's plan is not going to work out the way he thinks it will. I think the moment may come for him, as he walks toward the pin on the eighteenth for the hundredth time, when he wonders, "Is this all there is?" Recall that I mentioned this inevitable moment in chapter 6. I have seen countless men and women master the first three levels of building their business and then retire into nothingness. They finally have all they ever dreamed of, and *that* is the problem. The dream is over. Now what?

It is totally within your rights to have a business that is an ATM—just spitting out money without you having to do a thing. It is totally within your rights to start business after business and live within the first three levels of makin' money, takin' money, and sippin' on mai tais the whole time. But our good old buddy Maslow may roll his eyes if that is all we do, because we won't be living into self-actualization. For that to happen, you need to realize there are two more levels. I had no idea myself. I thought that once I had made my business run on automatic, I was done. Alas, it wasn't just a cannonball there, there was an entire city connected to it.

In April 2017, a local teen was walking through a field in Kansas and found a cannonball. An old cannonball. A very old cannonball. Local authorities notified archaeological experts, and it was immediately identified as a conquistador cannonball used in attacks against the indigenous population. What was subsequently found "under" the cannonball was the city of Eztanoas. An entire lost city of Native Americans, hiding away in Kansas.

That is what it will feel like when you experience the two highest levels of the Business Hierarchy of Needs (BHN), IMPACT and LEGACY. These levels are the size of a city, compared to the three foundational levels. Because it is at these highest levels that the business and *you* transform from getting to giving. This is where you have the realization that you are on the planet to contribute in some unique fashion, specific to you. This is where you realize you have the opportunity of a lifetime. As an entrepreneur you have been given the platform to influence countless others and to do it on a permanent basis.

A big mind-set and perhaps moral shift happens at these levels. You must first master the basic levels of SALES, PROFIT, and OR-DER. Then realize that you have a power you can now use for the greater good of your community, your country, our world. Then de-cide whether you want to play at this level.

When you are out to transform and build a legacy, the business will start to get even stronger in sales, profit, and order, because as the Blues Brothers would say you're ". . . on a mission from God."

IMPACT and LEGACY matter, but only the day you make a mental shift. If you are satisfied and fulfilled as a business owner accumulating wealth and comfort . . . that is totally cool . . . and that means you are best served by playing just the first three levels of the BHN. However, if you have a shift (like I have), and you realize there is something much bigger happening, then you are ready to play all five levels. If right now you are asking "Is this all there is?" then you are definitely ready for IMPACT and LEGACY.

It ain't just a cannonball, compadre. There is a whole booming metropolis waiting for you to discover.

Legacy, as I define it, is not about how much money you have, and it's not about fame or power. Legacy may be accomplished just as effectively through the distribution of wealth as by whispering the words someone needs to hear at precisely the moment they need to hear them. Legacy doesn't require you to have accumulated millions, or even thousands, though if you want to you can use millions (or thousands) to sustain it. Legacy is not about you. It is about what you leave behind.

Legacy for a business is all about the business continuing to have impact beyond your active participation. This is when you realize that the business your started and grew and served and did everything within your power to make successful was never really about you. This is when you realize that the business was about having a positive impact on our world. This is the point at which you realize that your job is to have it live on without you. And this is when you realize that you never really "owned" the business; you have always been its steward.

Who founded Coca-Cola? No Googling! No, the founder was not Dr Pepper. I bet you don't know who the founder was off the top of your head, and you probably don't care. That doesn't mean that Asa Griggs Candler had failed to leave a legacy. We all know Coca-Cola continues today stronger than ever, and so Candler was a massive legacy success. Apple continues without Steve Jobs. Mary Kay marches forward without Mary Kay. Dale Carnegie's trainings go on without him. Levi's, Walmart, and countless other companies live on long after their founders moved on, or passed away—and that is exactly what the founders wanted.

At the LEGACY level of the BHN, the business is linked to the mission and purpose of the organization, and not the founder. That mission and purpose may have originated with the founder, but it is no longer *associated* with the founder. In other words, legacy has everything to do with you and nothing to do with you. You founded your company, you built it through blood, sweat, and tears, and now your job is to ensure it lives on long after you have left it behind. It may even live on long after you have left this earth.

As a leader, you define how you want your company to change the world (IMPACT) and how you will ensure that mission will forevermore be fulfilled without you (LEGACY).

Need #1: Community Continuance

Question: Do your clients fervently defend, support, and help the business?

I remember my last call with Burt Shavitz, the cofounder and face of Burt's Bees, the $1 billion skin-care company that started with their famed beeswax lip balm. He was an eccentric guy, to say the least. He didn't have a phone at his tiny cabin in Maine, and he didn't have a cell phone. To reach Burt, I had to call the local diner in his town on a specific day at a specific time and ask if Burt was around and available to talk. We spoke a few times, and I shared his fascinating growth strategies in my book *Surge*. It was in those conversations that I learned more about how he and his business partner, Roxanne Quimby, started the company, and how he ended up selling his shares to her for a mere $130,000. At the time we spoke, he was effectively removed from Burt's Bees fully, except for his likeness, which was still used to sell the brand. The company had been acquired by Clorox for $925 million, and he was stuck in a nasty lawsuit with his former business partner.

On our last call, Burt lamented what had become of his company. It was a big juggernaut corporate machine now and, in his opinion, had lost the essence of what Burt believed in: simplicity.

Before we hung up for the last time, I asked, "Burt, if you could do it all over again, what would you do?"

"I wouldn't do it," he said.

I can't think of a more succinct way to put it. If you don't define and prepare for your legacy, it will still happen. Just not the way you want it to.

Legacy is not about going public or making billions. Legacy is about intentionally leaving your mark in the way you envision. How do you want to see the world changed, even if your world is simply your community or friends? At the LEGACY level of the BHN, you are defining what you want to leave as your mark, setting up a structure for that to happen, and then making your exit—on your terms.

Burt passed away in July 2015. The community who loved Burt, the real Burt, was not the community buying Burt's Bees from Clorox. The new "Cloroxed" Burt's Bees customers weren't rallying to bring back the simplicity that Burt was all about. There was no outrage as the brand abandoned its founding ideals. If the quality of the product slips, customers will simply abandon it rather than rally to help fix it. It is just a brand name, and perhaps one that will be successful for decades to come. It just wasn't what Burt wanted.

OMEN: Community Continuance

Let's pretend you are the founder and CEO of Smoketastic Smokers. You make great electric smoker grills that can cook the most tender meats in the world. Your SALES, PROFIT, ORDER, and IMPACT all show this. However, your Fix This Next analysis points to the fact that there is no community per se. Until now. OMEN time.

1. *Objective:* You believe that great meals are at the core of great families. As they say, "A family that eats together, stays together." Regardless of your business, you want this important message to live on forever. You know you have an opportunity for your business to be the torch that your clients carry.

2. *Measurement:* One thing you have seen other successful brands do is evolve into communities. BMW and Harley-Davidson both have rallies. The game developer Blizzard has their fabled BlizzCon, which is the "most epic family reunion on the planet." And even the Flat Earth Society has its annual wackos meetup, somewhere near the edge of the planet apparently. So you want to measure the number of gatherings your customers have in which your product is front and center. Family reunions? Tailgate parties? Food festivals?

3. *Evaluation:* This is something that will take time to develop. You decide that your own annual event may be the starting point.

4. *Nurture:* You bring your team up to speed on the plan and seek critical feedback. You agree that you need a board of advisers, select customers who are vocal or versed or both in your smokers. Then, you get to planning your first annual event, "the Great Smoketastic Family Reunion." Your goal is to have smoking contests, music, activities, and all of it focused on a family-friendly time.

5. *Result:* The first event is a small hit, with one hundred people attending. The turnout was way short of what you had hoped, but the talk afterward was worth it. Apparently, an impromptu session of sharing broke out at the event: backyard chefs shared recipes that can only be made in a Smoketastic smoker. That's when you saw the first site pop up online: chefs started sharing their recipes and family stories. As reunions got bigger and bigger, it was what was happening on the sidelines that was the real stuff. The magic happened at your third reunion, when a member of your tribe decided to declare a new "family dinner" national holiday and led the charge. Legacy launched—by your community! Even as your firm released new models and discontinued old ones, "smoketorians" started forums about preserving old models to serve family dinners for years or decades to come. You have become the Airstream of smokers, because of your community. The legacy is set to live on.

Need #2: Intentional Leadership Turn

Question: Is there a plan for leadership to transition and stay fresh?

A couple of years after the revised and expanded edition of *Profit First* came out, I was invited to be the closing keynote at a major business conference, with well over ten thousand people in attendance. Before I speak I like to get a feel for an event and audience. So when I can, I will visit the conference for a few hours and blend into the crowd. It probably won't surprise you that few people typically recognize me before I go onstage. I am an author, after all. They may recognize a book title, but not the picture of the guy in a vest buried on the inside flap of a dustjacket. After a speech, though, that is when *everyone* recognizes you, because you were just onstage.

At this particular conference, I sat down next to a fellow who (no surprise) didn't recognize me. When I settled into my seat, he tapped me on the shoulder.

"I don't think we've met before," he said in a hushed tone. "What kind of work do you do?"

"I'm an author," I responded in an elevated whisper.

His eyes lit up and he said, "You've *got* to read this amazing book called"—wait for it . . . waaaaait for it—"*Profit First.*"

My heart filled up and my ego did a dance for joy. Ha! This supercool guy I just met is recommending my own book *to me*, I thought. I couldn't wait to drop the bomb that he was talking to the author guy himself. Oh, the surprise I was about to see on his face.

Before my big fat ego could reveal I wrote the book, he interjected, "It's written by Cyndi Thomason."

Big pointy needle? Check. Big fat ego balloon? Check. Pop goes the big fat ego balloon.

Whoa. I'd written the book—twice—and presented the methodology thousands of times, and this super-jerk-wad guy thought someone else wrote it. I was stunned and my stupid, fat ego was crushed—for about a minute. Then something shifted in me, and I was filled with delight. The balloon started to soar.

You see, Cyndi is a Profit First Professional (PFP)* and the author of *Profit First for eCommerce*, one of the Profit First supplemental books focused on niche markets. Cyndi is also one of the PFPs who is trained and authorized to give my speech—yes, the same content—at her own and other events.

I thanked the wonderful man for his (excellent) recommendation, and then made my way backstage. As I waited to go on, I realized I had goosebumps all over my arms. I was pumped that Profit First was an idea spreading beyond me. I was excited that others were now leading the idea. Profit First today belongs as much to me as it does to Cyndi Thomason, John Briggs, Shawn Van Dyke, Chris Anderson, Drew Hinrichs, Katie Marshall, Mike McLenahan, and many others who are writing authorized niche Profit First books and/or going onstage spreading the word.

That day, at that event, is when I realized I am simply a steward of Profit First. It belongs to the world now.

You know you've created a legacy when you've let go of ownership and you get more excitement out of how the idea is serving people than you do being attached to it.

To be clear, I don't let other PFPs or anyone else take my idea and say it's their own. That's plagiarism and theft. Sadly, I actually had to take legal action against a company that purported to be the creators of Profit First. Those people are thieves. Cyndi is not; she is a steward too. I love that she is out there sharing the process

---

*Profit First Professionals is an organization of accountants, bookkeepers, and coaches who are certified in the Profit First methodology. To learn more visit ProfitFirstProfessionals .com.

with proper attribution, and I love that accounting and business professionals with niche expertise are taking to the foundational concept I developed and creating fresh ideas and adaptations of it. I want Profit First to be part of a journey of ever-expanding improvement for entrepreneurs. The fact that some super-awesome-rando guy thought Cyndi wrote my book is proof that that is already happening.

Do you have a plan for people to take over leadership when you move on? How will your innovative ideas spread without you? These are the questions you must ask yourself if you are going to fulfill this basic LEGACY need.

OMEN: Intentional Leadership Turn

In this hypothetical sitch, let's pretend you have an ad agency. Ten years in, and with a consistent tenacity in fixing the right things at the right time in your business, it has grown to have a strong foundation all the way from SALES to LEGACY. You love working for it, but there is one thing you love more: giving your clients (which are almost all small businesses) the upper hand in advertising over the big players in the market. Your goal is to make sure your business can continue to deliver on your promise, even if you are not there. OMEN time!

1. *Objective:* You intend to have an ad agency that continues to grow and serve its legacy, regardless of the leader. You have set the mission to give small businesses a big advantage. You

have thirty-five employees now, and need to set up a plan
for leaders to step in and step up.

2. *Measurement:* This is less about timing than it is about
preparation. You don't have a plan to retire anytime soon,
but you also realize life's circumstances change on a dime,
and for the business to continue it must be ready. So the first
metric is, do you have a plan? And the next metric is, are
you executing on it?

3. *Evaluation:* This process will not happen overnight, but a
plan can be put together quickly. You set interim goals for a
bullet point of objectives, then a leadership transition plan,
then candidates to groom, and ultimately a new leader to
introduce. You read up on the pros and cons of transitions,
such as General Electric's transition from Jack Welch to Jeff
Immelt. Outwardly it looked good, but inwardly it was
fraught with ego and conflict. You try to glean what you can,
implement the stuff that worked, and establish parameters
to avoid transitional conflict.

4. *Nurture:* This is a team effort, with all your leaders involved.
Transition means that many people shift. The constant
question you bring to your team is, how can we keep our
mission solid and our executive team fluid? Some suggest a
term of presidency, like a democratic country. As nice as
that sounds, this is not a democracy. Your team concludes
that the people within, who have lived the mission and
have the capability to be groomed, will be the best subse-
quent leaders. Your team looks into the story of Kat Cole,

the former Hooters waitress who went on to be the vice president of Hooters. She then became president of Cinnabon for four years, before being promoted to president of the company that owns Cinnabon, along with other brands like Moe's and Auntie Anne's.

5. *Result:* The process is in place and the potential leaders have been identified. But you are still running the show and will for the foreseeable future. After all, you love what you do, and the business is the best in its space. The new leaders are being groomed so well that if they don't have an opportunity to replace you within the next five years, they will be introduced to other companies by you, to be considered to lead them. Your goal isn't to keep them in waiting, but to continue to develop leaders for companies who want to build their own positive legacy, and to have a few people who are ready when your company needs a new leader.

Need #3: Heart-based Promoters

Question: Is the organization promoted by individuals inside and outside the organization, without need of direction?

Have you ever watched the show *Brooklyn Nine-Nine*? It's a comedy about the 99th Precinct in Brooklyn starring Andy Samberg, the guy who got famous doing the funny video shorts on *Saturday Night Live*. *Brooklyn Nine-Nine* was picked up by Fox in 2013, and although they earned critical acclaim and had a cult following, the network cancelled the show after five seasons.

On May 11, 2018, when news of the cancellation broke, devoted fans took to social media in droves. They created a hashtag on Twitter—#SaveB99—and relentlessly posted about the show on multiple platforms. They also started a petition calling on Fox to change its mind. Lin-Manuel Miranda, the creator of the Broadway hit *Hamilton*, got in on it, as well as many other notable fans. On May 12—just one day after the cancellation—the show's creator announced that NBC had picked up *Brooklyn Nine-Nine*. The fans had saved their show.

The point here is that the community was carrying the business now. It wasn't Andy Samberg coordinating a protest. It wasn't the show's producers asking the audience to sign a petition. It was the audience itself who would not let the show go away.

Of late, we've seen television shows from years past get reboots: *Full House* and *Will and Grace*, for example. That's some next-level fan power. Would those shows be back on the air years after cancellation if their fans were not still watching reruns and participating in fan events online and offline? Nope. Thanks to Netflix and other streaming services, older shows have new, young audiences.

I got to thinking about the link between active generations of fans when I went to see Marc Freedman's presentation. He's the author of *How to Live Forever*, and his entire speech was about building relationships that span generations. I had expected him to talk about advancements in stem-cell research, hormone replacement, different biochemical and genetic techniques, and a little dose of "exercise more and eat cleaner." Instead, he focused on studies that show that having relationships with younger generations extends life expectancy of both younger and older generations.

As Marc completed his speech, it became clear to me that successful businesses (businesses with longevity) also connect generations deliberately—generations of *consumers*. That connection is anchored through love and affection. The question is, how do you shower your clients with love and affection so that your business will continue on for generations? How do you have them actively and excitedly brag about their connections with you? You do it through stories. You do it through symbols. You do it through specialized lingo. You do it through congregation points.

Disneyland is all about family fun, and Mickey Mouse is a representation of that. Heart-based fans carry on the message by wearing the symbol, and those of other Disney characters. The congregation points are the theme parks. Starbucks has the congregation points, which are their stores. They have their own lingo, like, "venti, grande, frappawhatsit." They have their symbols and colors and look. All of that makes the loyalists become more loyal. They start bringing the Starbucks vibe to their own homes. At our house, we have Starbucks mugs, Starbucks coffee, and I dare say my wife has a Starbucks shirt (or ten).

For all that is holy, Harley-Davidson has people tattooing their freaking body with the company's logo. Jimmy Buffett has people drinking really shitty margaritas (trust me, I know my margaritas) at their Margaritaville bars, because people have become "parrot heads"—the unique language of the community. CrossFit has their own stuff, lingo, and congregation points. So does *Saturday Night Live*, Southwest Airlines, and the list goes on. Every one of these brands has a community of heart-based followers, people who see

the greater good and impact the business is having and feel com- ▼
pelled to spread the word. They become evangelists. ▼

Television, film, and literary communities thrive on fans who ▼
self-identify as part of a show's "fandom." Fan communities have ▼
online spaces where they write fan fiction about their show. They ▼
have conventions (cons) where they dress up like the characters
and meet the actors and show creators.

A quick shout-out to my boy Maslow for this one. In his human
hierarchy of needs, he pointed out the importance of belonging.
The third level of his hierarchy is the need to be in a community, to
be part of something. Successful brands create a unique community
for their clients. These companies, through their actions and what
they stand for, are showering their customers with love and affection and belonging. At the end of the day, that is what people really
want. And when they get it from a good company, or a television
show, they will shout it from the rooftops, because they are part of
something.

OMEN: Heart-based Promoters

In this scenario, let's say you found a museum of oddities and pecu-
liarities. A little like Ripley's Believe It or Not, but with a spin.
Every oddity you collect represents some form of triumph. It could
be nature, or human, or other, but in every case your pieces achieve
an unexpected win. One of them is a doll dressed in a gas mask,
which was found at the Chernobyl nuclear disaster. The win in this
case is nature. Scientists originally estimated it would take twenty

thousand years before life would return to the site. But after only thirty years, wildlife is thriving there. Even with a catastrophic human disaster, Mother Nature found a way to rebound. You love the message of triumph, and know for the museum to live on, your patrons have to want to spread the word.

1. *Objective:* Make the message of triumph the legacy. Do this by empowering your community to spread the message of the museum and, more important, do it on their own accord.

2. *Measurement:* This is something you'll experience in the ether of the internet. You will likely see other indications too, like increased museum visits. It is unclear in advance, so you plan to put an ear to the ground as you proceed and measure whatever presents itself. As you evaluate your progress, you will likely nurture the measurements to achieve your objective.

3. *Evaluation:* It is difficult to pick a time frame because you don't really have any sense of how long it will take for your objective to come true. And you don't know how to measure it well. So the plan is simply to get started, then to discuss your observations once a month.

4. *Nurture:* You talk with your curation team on how to get the community taking ownership of what you do, and two genius ideas come together. One is to encourage patrons to take on a new label: Triumph Curators. At the completion of a museum tour, the patron is given a small pamphlet inviting them to take on that role for your museum. Their job is to identify new potential exhibit ideas from around the world, notify your museum, and even help procure the items when possible

(and permitted). The second idea blends in perfectly with the first. When an item is curated, the exhibit gets a permanent thank-you plaque giving attribution to them.

5. *Result:* Most people don't want to be curators, they just want to see weird stuff. But a select few, or better said, a self-selected few, see the greater mission of the goodness that comes out of your museum—that it is not about weird stuff, but about unexpected paths to triumph. Those people step into their new volunteer roles. While museum visits are increasing, it is not indicative of your museum establishing the permanence that you want, but something else is. It is clear that the Triumph Curators are taking the title seriously. You see them starting their own websites about their work, and one site has become so popular that it has translated into a full-time business for that Triumph Curator. After three years, more items are curated by community than your team, and you are confident that you have established a museum that will grow from the community. The fact that at least one more business has launched on your inspirational theme is the greatest indicator that you have a legacy in the making.

Need #4: Quarterly Dynamics

Question: Does your business have a clear vision for its future and dynamically adjust quarterly to make that vision become true?

Quarterly dynamics is the simple concept of adjusting to the parameters around your business every ninety days, to most efficiently move toward your objective. Similar to the tacking method used by sailors to capture the wind (energy) around their sailboat, quarterly dynamics is a method to regularly realign all the elements of your business. In short, tacking is where you first define your target—perhaps an island a few miles out in the ocean. Then you set your sails to leverage the winds to move most directly toward the island, also while navigating around obstacles such as sandbars, other crafts, and that monster mother shark from *Jaws 3-D* that ate boats whole. After a short distance, you realign the boat by turning in the other direction, enough to fully capture the wind, and push forward again toward the island. This time, though, the boat is offset on a new angle, again leveraging the wind (and avoiding obstacles). It does this continuously to zigzag its way to the island. Using tacking, the sailboat gets to the island every time, though not in a straight line. So it is in business: we may want to travel a direct path toward our goals, but in reality it's more of a zigzag as we leverage the winds (the market) and navigate around obstacles (competitors, the economy, etc.).

To master the LEGACY level, your business must be able to reinvent and realign itself. Look at LEGO, the toy company famous for captivating children with colorful interlocking blocks with which they can build the firehouses and pirate ships of their dreams—and for causing parents to curse loudly (directly in front of their children, mind you) when they step on one of those tiny little plastic implements of pain. LEGO has been around since 1932, yet in the late 1990s they were close to bankruptcy. This was in part because people viewed their line of LEGO building sets as a thing of the past, marketed primarily to boys, and they could not compete with the fast-changing toy market.

LEGO improved its systems and cut costs, and then in 2011 they revamped their brand to be more inclusive. Now their sets appealed to both boys and girls. Then came the movie—*The Lego Movie*. Way to title, LEGO. That movie changed everything. Aside from earning nearly half a billion dollars worldwide, the movie and its sequel positioned the company to be more than just a toy brand. Now it was a franchise. Bloomberg noted that in 2015 LEGO had a revenue increase of 31 percent, roughly about $1.34 billion.

OMEN: Quarterly Dynamics

Welcome to your hypothetical company in need of a little help: Ice Me Tea. You make some of the best iced tea in the country, that can't be denied. Your sales are strong, your profit is predictable, you have mastered all the needs at the ORDER level, and you are transforming lives. You do this by making iced tea into almost a ceremony, similar to sharing coffee with a friend. The challenge now is stagnation. The Fix This Next analysis pinpoints to the need to have leadership embrace quarterly dynamics throughout the organization. Let's OMEN this!

1. *Objective:* To prevent stagnation in not just your product, but in any part of your organization. This will require each department to develop its own quarterly dynamic plan. Every part of your business must be able to adjust dynamically yet cohesively to the greater organization.
2. *Measurement:* This one, happily, is simple. Does each distinct department have a quarterly dynamic plan in place? This is a

ninety-day plan that moves them closest to their overarching goals. At the end of these ninety-day "bursts," the departments resync to see how their actions are supporting (or hampering) each other, and then make adjustments.

3. *Evaluation:* As the leader of the organization you must actively support communication, harmony, and productive arguing between departments. So your rhythm is actually weekly check-ins to make sure communication is flowing, then ninety-day check-ins to make sure the company departments are making the right zigs and zags to elevate the company as a whole.

4. *Nurture:* This is a leadership opportunity. You communicate the grand vision to the leaders of the departments and discuss the vision and get commitment. Then you must structure metrics to support the achievement of the grand vision with full support from each department, while also emphasizing the importance of departments to support each other, even if it means delaying their own objectives to help another achieve theirs and elevate the company vision.

5. *Result:* This takes a lot of active communication, and as the leader of your company you have two big roles: the chief cheerleader and the chief communicator. You keep preaching the mission like you are beating a drum and you keep everyone talking about helping everyone succeed. Then the magic happens. Your sales department takes a hit in sales objectives because the service department has an unexpected hiccup. The sales department was on track to have its best year ever, but equipment failures in service caused

long delays and dissatisfied customers. So the sales department intentionally slowed sales and redirected clients elsewhere because that was in the best interest of both the customer and the service department. A great tack around a big potential problem. To most leaders, cheering on your sales department when sales dip seems nothing short of strange. But to you, the fact that sales is more concerned about the company's overall success and reputation over simply hitting the numbers proves you have team players through and through.

Need #5: Ongoing Adaptation

Question: Is the business designed to constantly adapt and improve, including finding ways to better and best itself?

Everything that is working for your business now will likely stop working at some point and need to be replaced by something new—a new approach, new technology or equipment, or new roles in your company. The typewriter yielded to the keyboard, which will ultimately give way to voice-to-text translators, which may give way to the fruits of the research being done right now on thought-to-text, or something else we can't even imagine at this juncture. The question is, is your business prepared for hard or impossible-to-predict change? You can't leave a legacy if your company dies because it is unprepared for the unexpected.

As an author, I want to assume that books will be around for centuries more, but that thinking is a trap. Just because something has been around for centuries already—or is well-established in some other way—does not mean that it will continue. This is why I'm experimenting with one-on-one connection, ways that readers can access me directly to get their unique questions answered. Right now, it's that affirmation loop of emails sent to me hourly. And yet, responding to hundreds of emails daily is not sustainable. I'm not sure how I'll pull it off, but the point is, I'm considering it. I'm pondering the question and experimenting with solutions. I'm not expecting anything to remain unchanged.

My mind goes right to Netflix. Netflix originally delivered movies via mail and transitioned to on-demand over the internet. They continue to morph as they now make movies downloadable to your smart devices so you can watch on your tablet as you fly. This in turn has triggered changes for airlines. Fewer and fewer planes have embedded screens, as they swap them out with special holders for your smart device, on which you can watch your downloaded Netflix videos, or live television through the plane's wi-fi. I suspect one day, Netflix (or some other company that morphs) will have some kind of implant that goes right into your brain so you can experience the movie by being part of it. *Total Recall*–style. The one constant is change.

Nintendo morphed from a playing-card manufacturer to a video-game-console leader. Wrigley's transitioned from a soap company to a gum company. And NASCAR's humble beginnings came from moonshiners needing a way to get their stash of illegal booze away from the cops in fast cars, and morphed into legal racing at ludicrous speeds in front of a hundred thousand people drinking moonshine.

The lesson is this: if you fail to change, you will fail. Therefore, change must be built into the essence of your business.

OMEN: Ongoing Adaptation

Congratulations! You finally have that bar you always dreamed of owning in this example. You call it the Fan Dome and it is a unique sports bar. It has a single massive screen modeled after a movie theater, and the seating is similar to two sections of a sports stadium. You enter at the top and walk down steps to bleacher seating on the left and the right. One side is for the home team and the other for visitors. The waiters serve food and drinks the way stadiums do it, walking the steps and yelling out "Get your cold one here," all while the big game plays on the megascreen.

Your Fix This Next analysis shows that your Vital Need is ongoing adaptation. Come on. You have one last OMEN in you. I know you do.

1. *Objective:* Your business idea is a big hit right out of the gate, because no other bar has done anything like this before. That said, for your business to become a legacy it needs to be ready for the unexpected and adjust accordingly.

2. *Measurement:* You have your quarterly dynamics plan in place for your leadership team and this is where you add one final major piece. You will not just be analyzing challenges and opportunities to move on in the next ninety days, you and your colleagues are going to look at the ultimate end goal you set. This is where you ask yourself and your team if

it is time to fully reinvent yourselves. To do this, you have a simple plan: Utopia Corp.

3. *Evaluate:* With your quarterly dynamic plan, now every ninety days you ask and vigorously argue, "Are we in the right business?" You expect to hear all sides, all ideas—the good, the bad, the ugly.

4. *Nurture:* Using the Utopia Corp. exercise, you have your team develop business plans for new phantom companies with one goal in mind, to wipe the Fan Dome right off the map. Each of these teams then pitches their plans to the entire group, sharing their unique strategies for Utopia Corp. to outperform the Fan Dome. It is the ultimate brainstorming session, pitting your company against itself. One idea is solid: not all games get balanced attendance. Sometimes you get 90 percent or more of fans from one team. So a Utopia Corp. idea is to set up adjustable aisle banisters so the highly represented team gets a bigger section. Another idea is a game changer: your team notices that a lot of alumni associations gather at your bar and fill up the stands fully, wanting to get as close to a stadium experience as possible. You work on getting alumni cheerleaders in uniform to cheer on the fans, and in exchange they get free food and drink. The business is morphing and making stadiumlike events without the need to trek to the stadium.

5. *Result:* The repeating process shows that you don't need to revamp the business in its entirety, but it does trigger ideas such as "rewarding" fans for wearing team gear, getting cheer-leaders pumping up the crowd, and setting up security for the

few games at which people can get hostile. While there is no
red flag run up the pole showing the need for a total revamp
of the business (yet), the fact that you are working the quarterly dynamic plan every ninety days gives you and your leadership comfort that you are looking farther down the road
than your competitors.

Fix This Next in Action

Daa-bling. My phone received a text from Mike Agugliaro. He's the
founder of CEO Warrior, a high-end training and implementation organization for service-business owners, including HVAC, plumbing,
and electrical companies. I opened up the text and there was a picture
of the Hulk flexing and roaring. *Daa-bling.* The follow-up text from
Mike read: "This is game-changing stuff, Mike. This is the best system
I have ever seen from you."

I had just delivered a speech on Fix This Next to a VIP group of
business owners, and Mike was in the audience. He's hired me to
keynote his CEO Warrior event about three times a year for the
past ten years, so he knows my work inside out. I have presented
Profit First ten plus times, *Clockwork* five times, *The Pumpkin Plan*
five times, and a mix of my other books and concepts. Mike sits in
every time—even on the tenth presentation of *Profit First*. He listens and takes a relentless stream of notes.

This was the first time that Mike had seen me talk about Fix
This Next. I introduced the BHN, and instantly he was scribbling
away, asking questions, and sharing his thoughts. He committed to
doing the Fix This Next analysis, right there at the event. That's

how Mike rolls—identify the one thing that will have the biggest positive impact on his business and take immediate action on it (sound familiar?).

The next morning I got an email that detailed how he used the hierarchy, what he discovered, and the action he was taking. It read:

> The hierarchy is gold! It was extremely helpful in giving me clarity on our next opportunities for growth. I love how visual it is and have pinned it above my desk.
>
> Before I went through the BHN, I believed we needed to improve our leadership and management team's vision and communication, and build enhanced structures (such as improved organizational charts and streamlined processes).
>
> Going through the chart, I affirmed what I believed to be true. We have SALES, PROFIT, and ORDER nailed. I have a predictable business. But I am a guy who never wants my business to just be an ATM machine so I can goof off every day. I want to change lives, or as you put it, transform lives. We have the IMPACT phase nailed. Our customers become believers in what we are teaching, not just doers of what we teach. And with that commitment, we are transforming business after business.
>
> Now I see that LEGACY is where we are. How do I set up my business to forever change lives, without its dependency on me? I could see that:

Based on the questions in the chart, we have the following realization/awareness of LEGACY:

- We are achieving the first and fifth points of LEGACY (community continuance and ongoing adaptation) very well already.

- We're okay at the second, third, and fourth points of LEGACY, but see the opportunity to improve—especially clarifying our leadership transition plan, growing our community of promoters, and clarifying our vision for the future.

It affirmed what we already knew but provided clarity by narrowing our focus within the LEGACY level to the subcategories we do well versus the opportunities to improve. Now, with this focused clarity, we'll build a plan to execute ferociously to solve the three pieces, starting with the first Vital Need I identified in LEGACY.

I also realize now that this is not a ladder, but a loop. We will work to fully achieve LEGACY in its entirety. Then, as we continue to grow, I recognize that in the future the larger versions of our business may need course adjustments at every level as we scale our sales, profit, order, impact, and legacy. Therefore, as we double in size, we will go back to every new niche we serve (that usually makes us $3 million to $5 million) to make sure we are on track, and that we are pursuing every opportunity at each level.

▼
▼
▼
▼
▼

I feel like I finally have a simple, living, breathing strategy. I will call upon this daily. And I will probably watch you deliver fifteen more speeches on it. I need you keynoting our next event on this. Entrepreneurs need to hear this stuff and, honestly, I want to take more notes.

I RARELY SEE Frank Minutolo anymore. He was my first-ever business coach, and helped me navigate the growth and sale of two of my companies. He no longer does business coaching, and as he lives out the twilight of his life he has devoted himself to helping children in need. I was able to sit down with him for breakfast at a local diner earlier this year. As we ate, we talked about his life's journey so far. He brought Konika, a Japanese company, to the United States and grew it to $100 million in annual revenue. He coached dozens of entrepreneurs. He had an amazing wife as a best friend.

I said, "Frank, you have been so successful. That must bring you joy."

He looked at me and said, "Success has brought me pride. Working with at-risk children, that is bringing me joy." He then paused and added, "You may be successful, but will you matter?"

My eyes—and heart—opened that day. That is it. Success, as I desire it, is creating something that impacts others and has the ability to continue to deliver the impact long after I depart. That is how I define legacy. Perhaps you will choose the same definition. Do something that matters, and set it up to continue long after your twilight years.

YOU CAN AND YOU WILL

TOMAS GORNY HAS ONE OF THOSE AMERICAN DREAM STORIES THAT would make for a good movie. Born in Zabrze, Poland, he moved to the United States in his early twenties to pursue that dream. Tomas was broke, and he had a thick Polish accent that made some people assume he was "slow." He would get stuck on some English words, and mispronounce others, and so prejudices and assumptions kicked in. However, Tomas used those prejudices and assumptions as an advantage.

"Just because I speak slowly does not mean I think slowly," he told me.

Tomas applied a "rope-a-dope" strategy. Competitors would disregard Tomas's ability to meet or better their offers, and share "secrets" out of cockiness. Just when the other guy thought he had the best of "slow" Tomas, Tomas would come back with terms that gave him the best deal.

Tomas went on to grow multiple, multihundred-million-dollar

companies, and then sold them. He went from broke to billions, and now he is focused on his legacy. He has something to prove: the American Dream is real and accessible to all of us.

Currently, Tomas operates Nextiva, a VoIP company. When you walk the floors of this $350 million business, you'll see a relaxed environment full of humble employees . . . some with heavy accents . . . who are really, really smart. They have earned the right to walk around with their egos front and center. However, they are modeling Tomas, staying focused on getting the best deal; they are not worried what other people think of them.

Tomas and his team understand something that I want you to pay special attention to: The BHN is not a ladder that you climb. It is more like bicycle pedals. You push the pedal that will turn the gears, and which pedal you need to push switches back and forth. At times you brake, and at times you coast, but you have to work the pedals to move forward.

Here's how the BHN has played out for Nextiva:

Sales

- Tomas identified a product that could empower small businesses: phone systems. This was rooted to his mission—the small guy (the "slow" guy) needed a way to compete with the big guy (the bully). Yes, VoIP existed, but a sophisticated phone system that was as good, if not better, than the big corporate systems was a leg up.
- When Nextiva started, Tomas ran it out of an office the size of a minivan. All his focus was on how to get someone to be

the first buyer. Hint, for any new business, the first client is almost always the hardest, but Nextiva secured the clients it needed to move forward.

Profit

- With sustainable sales, Nextiva ensured their profitability structure was sound. This was something that was considered from their very first sale. But as the SALES level was achieved, Tomas dug deeper and deeper into the PROFIT level to ensure that they had optimized the pricing to be competitive and bring permanent profits. Nextiva competes with all the big VoIP providers, such as Verizon and Ring-Central. As of this writing, they are now the third largest VoIP provider in the United States.

- Even as Nextiva ensured the PROFIT level was strong, they went back to enhancing the SALES level to access a new market. Nextiva built alliances with systems integrators (computer and phone companies), where one strong relationship could bring in dozens if not hundreds of new clients.

Order

- As Nextiva tackled the ORDER level, they introduced efficiencies throughout the organization. One of my favorites was in the sales department. When you walk the sales floor (yes, it is an entire floor of people, nearly a couple of hundred on my last count), there are huge monitors on the walls reporting real-time metrics. Who is leading sales for the day? How are the teams doing? Who landed the most recent deal? Instead of a manager calling meetings and telling people how they are doing for the day, the reporting is automated and people stay motivated and on track.

Impact

- This goes back to the mission of Nextiva. I know this because I have been a user of their phone systems for ten years now, and I get out to their offices a few times a year to share my experience with their phones. I'm now part of the company's small advisory group.

- Messaging is consistent. Tomas and team Nextiva intend to always back up the little guy. Have you ever been at risk of getting involved in a fifth-grade schoolyard fight with the big bully targeting you, and then that really big kid from eighth grade walks over? You know, the one kid who hit puberty already, is ripped with muscles, and has a beard . . . on his chest? That kid walks over and taps you on the back and says, "I got this." That kid. He tells the bully to take a hike and he better never see him around you again and the bully runs away. That is what Nextiva does for small business.

Legacy

- Nextiva will live on long after Tomas is on to other things, because they are looking for ways to compete with themselves. As I am writing this, Nextiva is creating its second generation of its NextOS, a CRM and phone combo. The phone and CRM are one. Email, phone, texting, social media, all communication is unified with the client's profile so that it builds a history of the relationship with the client/prospect, and AI determines where the relationship is going and how to best manage it.

Perhaps you, too, have experienced prejudice in business. Maybe people have made assumptions about you and your abilities. Maybe you have made them about yourself. Like Tomas, you are not defined by other people's perceptions, or even your own fears about whether or not you can pull off the American Dream for your family, your staff, and yourself.

I'm here to tell you that you can. And you will.

Now you have the tool that will help you create sustained, healthy growth; the tool that will make it easy for you to figure out exactly which area of your business to focus on first, and exactly which problem to fix next. The BHN is the tool, the compass, that makes mastery *inevitable*—as long as you use it.

If you have been in business for months, years, or decades, that time is proof that you have mastered (or are on your way to mastering) the hundreds of elements that make a successful business. You have attracted prospects and turned them into clients. You have delivered your products or services. You have collected money and paid vendors. You have successfully navigated difficult employees, difficult clients, and difficult days. You have won business over the competition and celebrated, and you have lost business to the competition and got back up and pushed your business forward again.

I am certain that you have the skill and drive to move the business through any challenge. The fact that you have achieved what you have achieved makes you a superhero in my mind. If I got stuck out in the proverbial wild, I think I would want you as my survival companion. You have the drive to keep marching through the dry spells of the desert. You have the strength to cut through the thick, dark forest of distraction. You have the energy to climb the mountains, and you have the courage to face any beast that comes our way.

There are infinite ways to address business challenges—that part is up to you. As long as you know which way to turn, you'll get to your destination. You will find a way. I know you have it in you.

Imagine taking your power and channeling it in a specific direction instead of jumping back to the same things as yesterday. Imagine the distance you can cover. Imagine what you can discover in your journey, if you only had a tool that directed you forward, consistently.

Your business is the greatest platform for self-expression and to be of service. It is a powerful force that, when channeled, will deliver the most miraculous experiences to you. I hope that the knowledge you gained in this book becomes your most reliable navigation tool for your business, that it serves you for years to come, and that it serves the legacy of your business for generations to come. And like my friend Dave Rinn, whom I introduced you to in the opening of this book, I hope you pin the one simple sheet of the BHN above your desk. Or even just draw it on a piece of paper and keep it next to you as a reminder that when you are faced with the countless considerations of running your business, you take pause, find where your Vital Need is, and fix that next.

I am proud of you, my entrepreneurial friend. And I am humbled that you allowed me, even in just a small way, to be part of your journey.

ACKNOWLEDGMENTS

AJ'S EMAIL READ: "WE NEED A SOLID WEEKEND TOGETHER TO WRITE the outline for *Fix This Next*. I booked us a 'quiet and remote' home in New York state."

Upon arrival, my writing partner, AJ Harper, and I opened the door to the house of horrors. The 1970s wood paneling was the only comforting part. But perhaps it was meant to be. The decor (or lack thereof), and the fear of venturing outside kept us focused on one thing: writing this book.

AJ was relentless in her commitment to make *Fix This Next* the best book it could be. She would repeat "How do we make this simpler?" and "How do we make this better?" This book is not just the result of five years of research and writing, it is a result of a thirteen-year partnership between me and AJ. I can't think of a better writing partner and I surely can't think of a better friend. Thank you, AJ.

"It's Impact." Those simple words resolved the missing level in the Business Hierarchy of Needs. It was not my realization, but

Kelsey's. Kelsey "KRE" Ayres is the president of Obsidian Launch LLC, the holding company for the Mike Michalowicz brand. Kelsey is devoted to the eradication of entrepreneurial poverty. She leads our team as only Kelsey can, through kindness, generosity, and appreciation. It is my honor to work with you, Kelsey.

The experience of writing *Fix This Next* has been extraordinary, with one small exception: the day my editor, Kaushik Viswanath, called me to share a personal update. After working with me on *Profit First*, *Clockwork*, and *Fix This Next*, Kaushik decided to pursue a new position at a different company. This is a tough loss for Penguin, and a devastating one for me. Expect a dozen pink roses from me at your new digs. Partly because I miss you, and mostly because I like to embarrass you.

Thank you to Liz Dobrinska, my art director and website designer. She worked on the cover of this book, the design of my websites, and has been my exclusive brand consultant for more than fifteen years. Thank you for being with me through the highs and the lows, Liz. You're world-class.

Paul "2JU" Scheiter joined our team as a systems and process consultant. Not only is he a master engineer, he is the definition of an ultimate friend. He calls me out on my own shit, because he cares. I love you, Paul, you crazy smart redneck.

Thank you, Jeremey "J-Kablown" Smith, the other crazy redneck, for keeping the goof going and making sure our message on eradicating entrepreneurial poverty keeps getting out in new ways.

Thank you, Amy "Billy Ray Gumpersome" Cartelli, for your dedication to do whatever it takes to serve our company. You will always be the coolest "tier 1" girl I ever knew in high school, even though you called me "Mi-cal-low-shits."

You are a rock star, Jenna "Jememma" Lorenz. Thank you for managing all our communication with our readers. I can't imagine anyone doing the job better. Your secret? You care, a lot! By the way, I know you hate your nickname and that is why it stays.

Thank you to Lisa Pilazzi for scheduling all my speaking events, podcasts, webinars, TV appearances, and interviews. Well done, fire-fighter.

Amber Vilhauer! O.M.G. You are a machine! I'm awestruck by your devotion to the success of *Fix This Next*. Thank you from the bottom of my heart. I can't wait for your own book launch.

Thank you to Patti Zorr for being the "great documentor" of the *Fix This Next* marketing plan. You kept us on track and gave us amazing marketing ideas.

Thank you to Lillian Ball, my publicist at Penguin. Your willingness to work with our crazy marketing plans means the world to me.

Most importantly, so much gratitude goes to my wife, Krista Michalowicz. Thank you for supporting my dream of being an author and joining me on the journey. My latest request was: "Hey babe, I need to check out a house that has something like two hundred rooms. The woman who built it was running from evil spirits. I need to include a story about it in my book. I fly out tomorrow. Want to come?" Her response of "Hell yes!" is yet another confirmation that I married my best friend. I live you (not a typo).

FOUNDING FIXERS

	BUSINESS NAME	URL
Dr. Sabrina Starling	Tap the Potential LLC	https://www.tapthepotential.com/
Dean Carlson	Fit For Profit	https://fitforprofit.com/
Lee Collins	Repeat Profits, LLC	https://repeatprofits.com
Alison Beierlein	Alison Beierlein Small Business Consulting	https://www.alisonbeierlein.com/
Mark Coudray	Coudray Growth Technologies	http://www.coudray.com/
Ron Allen	Exigo Business Solutions	https://www.exigobusiness.com/
Shawn Walsh	Encore Strategic Consulting, LLC	https://encoresc.com/
Christeen Era and Dave Rinn	Core Growth Strategies	https://www.coregrowthstrategies.com/
Rob Foncannon	Foncannon CPA Group	https://www.foncannontax.com/

	BUSINESS NAME	URL
Brenda Batista-Mollohan	Inspiring Company Culture	https://www.inspiring companyculture.com/
Stuart Bryan	AutoCorrect Consulting, LLC	https://www.auto correctconsulting .com/
Azim Sahu-Khan	Business Performance Tuning	http://www.business performancetuning .com.au/
Billy Bush	Recode Strategy	https://recodestrategy .com
Linda Brown	Spire Business Inc.	https://spirebusiness .com/
Stacie Hays	Grace Ridge Finance	https://www.grace ridgefinance.com/
Karen Dellaripa	Beyond Your Books	http://beyondyour books.com/
Jillian Verdun	JMV Financial Services	https://www.jmv financialservices.com/
Kasey Anton	Spark Business Consulting	http://www.spark businessconsulting .com/
Toni Turner	The Business Planner	http://www.theb planner.com.au/
Alicia Laursen	Alicia's Accounting Associates, Inc	http://www.alicias accounting.com/

FTN GLOSSARY

Business Hierarchy of Needs (BHN): The BHN is loosely based on Maslow's hierarchy of needs and represents the five levels of business needs. Each foundational level must adequately support the needs at the level above it. The levels in order from the most essential needs to the highest needs: SALES, PROFIT, ORDER, IMPACT, AND LEGACY.

Certified Fix This Next Coach: A coaching professional who has taken advanced training and passed an annual certification exam in Fix This Next. A Certified Fix This Next Coach is skilled at advanced FTN procedures and is qualified to work with entrepreneurs on the FTN process. Go to FixThisNext.com for more info.

Clockwork: A book that details the process to make a business run on automatic, without the required active participation of the owner(s). The book documents the process of organizational efficiency, and identifies a four-week vacation as the litmus test for a business that can run without the owner.

Core Needs: A total of twenty-five needs over the five levels of the BHN, these represent the most fundamental needs that all businesses have.

Double Helix Trap: A term popularized by business author Barry Moltz. This is when your company's focus oscillates between sales and deliverables. The business is incapable of growing both simultaneously, and as a result the business growth is stagnated.

Entrepre-Joneses: Entrepreneurs whom other entrepreneurs feel compelled to keep pace with (even, or especially, when it is not financially healthy).

Fix This Next (FTN): A system to identify and resolve a company's needs in a sequence that will facilitate the fastest and healthiest growth.

FTN Analysis: A four-step process used to pinpoint a company's Vital Need. Once the Vital Need is fully resolved or is on a consistent/predictable path to resolution, the FTN analysis is repeated to find the next Vital Need.

Get Stage: The three base levels of the BHN, including SALES, PROFIT, and ORDER. At these three foundational levels the business creates money, stability, and efficiency so that it can sustain.

Give Stage: The two highest levels of the BHN, including IMPACT and LEGACY. At these two highest levels the business positions itself as a societal contributor that will stick around for the long haul.

Impact Level: The fourth level of the BHN, IMPACT is the creation of transformational experience for a company's clients, and even its employees and vendors. At this level the business moves from transactions alone, necessary at the prior three levels, to also bringing about transformation and greater meaning to the clients, employees, and vendors.

Legacy Level: The highest level of the BHN, LEGACY is the creation of permanence. The business structure is enhanced to "live on" beyond the ownership of the organization, and for the business to transform dynamically to the changing market.

Maslow's Hierarchy of Needs: A concept originally proposed by Abraham Maslow in 1943 as "A Theory of Human Motivation." It specifies five categories of human need. In order from the most essential need to the highest-level need, they are Physiological, Safety, Belongingness, Esteem, and Self-Actualization.

Old-Fashioned: My new libation love, and maybe yours too. Who knew something could compete with a margarita or a tequila gimlet? Enjoy a celebratory old-fashioned or liquid of your preference every time you resolve a Vital Need.

OMEN: A technique for defining, monitoring, and tweaking goals. OMEN is an acronym for the four steps:

1. Objective—Set the result you intend to achieve.
2. Measurement—Determine the way(s) you will measure progress toward your Objective.
3. Evaluation—Commit to the frequency that the measurements will be reviewed.
4. Nurture—Specify how you will tweak the Objective and/or the Measurement and/or the Evaluation should you not be achieving your intentions.

Order Level: The third level of the BHN, ORDER is the creation of efficiency throughout the organization. The business is free of dependency on any individual for its ongoing, healthy operation.

Profit First: A book and methodology by the same name that directs a business owner to take a predetermined percentage of income and allocate it as profit, remove the profit from the business, and operate the business off the remainder. This is the pay-yourself-first principle, applied to business.

Profit Level: The second level of the BHN, PROFIT is the retention of cash, which is created by sales. Profit brings stability to a business.

Sales Level: The base level of the BHN, SALES is necessary for a business to create cash.

Surge: A book that specifies a process to become an industry leader. Businesses that identify niche markets, monitor movements in that vertical, and create offerings in front of growing demand catch the wave of that space, therefore positioning the business to be the next industry authority.

Survival Trap: The result of responding to an apparent and urgent issue while unintentionally neglecting the considerations that will permanently move a business toward its vision. The Survival Trap is typified by the sensation of "taking two steps forward, then three steps back."

The Pumpkin Plan: A book that explains the process for explosive, organic growth. Using an analogy of colossal pumpkin farming, it explains that the removal of distracting clients (bad pumpkins) and concentrating specific offerings for specific niches results in strong, healthy growth.

The Toilet Paper Entrepreneur: A book for startups or struggling businesses, it details how to leverage insufficient resources to your greatest advantage. A lack of cash, a lack of experience, and a lack of clients is the best way to create resourceful, industry-changing opportunities.

Theory of Constraints: Popularized by Eli Goldratt in his book *The Goal*, it is the theory that a process can move only as quickly as the output of the bottleneck in the process.

Unchecked Core Need: A need that is not being satisfactorily served. A business will typically have multiple unchecked core needs at any given time. Of these, the Vital Need is identified as the most pressing unchecked core need at the lowest level of the BHN.

Vital Need: The most significant roadblock your company is currently experiencing. This is the element of your business you should fix next to facilitate healthy, fast growth. Once a Vital Need is fully resolved or is on a consistent/predictable path to resolution, use the FTN analysis to identify the Vital Need your company must address next.

THE *FIX THIS NEXT* 1-SHEET

STEP 1: Check the satisfied Core Needs

STEP 2: Identify the foundational Vital Need

STEP 3: Fix the Vital Need

STEP 4: With the Vital Need resolved, repeat the process

SALES ❑ Lifestyle Congruence ❑ Prospect Attraction ❑ Client Conversion
❑ Delivering on Commitments ❑ Collecting on Commitments

PROFIT ❑ Debt Eradication ❑ Margin Health ❑ Transaction Frequency
❑ Profitable Leverage ❑ Cash Reserves

ORDER ❑ Minimized Wasted Effort ❑ Role Alignment ❑ Outcome Delegation
❑ Linchpin Redundancy ❑ Mastery Reputation

IMPACT ❑ Transformation Orientation ❑ Mission Motivation
❑ Dream Alignment ❑ Feedback Integrity ❑ Complementary Network

LEGACY ❑ Community Continuance ❑ Intentional Leadership Turn
❑ Heart-based Promoters ❑ Quarterly Dynamics ❑ Ongoing Adaptation

2

The current level is: _____

With the Vital Need of: _____

3

Objective: _____
_____

Measurement(s): _____
_____

Evaluation: _____
_____

Nurture: _____
_____

4 Repeat this process once the Vital Need is fully resolved.

Take the FREE evaluation at FixThisNext.com   ©2019 Mike Michalowicz

THE 25 CORE NEEDS OF *FIX THIS NEXT*

SALES

☐ 1 - **Lifestyle Congruence:** Do you know what the company's sales performance must be to support your personal comfort?

☐ 2 - **Prospect Attraction:** Do you attract enough quality prospects to support your needed sales?

☐ 3 - **Client Conversion:** Do you convert enough of the right prospects into clients to support your needed sales?

☐ 4 - **Delivering on Commitments:** Do you fully deliver on your commitments to your clients?

☐ 5 - **Collecting on Commitments:** Do your clients fully deliver on their commitments to you?

PROFIT

☐ 1 - **Debt Eradication:** Do you consistently remove debt rather than accumulate it?

☐ 2 - **Margin Health:** Do you have healthy profit margins within each of your offerings and do you continually seek ways to improve them?

☐ 3 - **Transaction Frequency:** Do your clients repeatedly buy from you over alternatives?

☐ 4 - **Profitable Leverage:** When debt is used, is it used to generate predictable, increased profitability?

☐ 5 - **Cash Reserves:** Does the business have enough cash reserves to cover all expenses for three months or longer?

ORDER

☐ 1 - **Minimized Wasted Effort:** Do you have an ongoing and working model to reduce bottlenecks, slowdowns, and inefficiencies?

☐ 2 - **Role Alignment:** Are people's roles and responsibilities matched to their talents?

☐ 3 - **Outcome Delegation:** Are the people closest to the problem empowered to resolve it?

☐ 4 - **Linchpin Redundancy:** Is your business designed to operate unabated when key employees are not available?

☐ 5 - **Mastery Reputation:** Are you known for being the best in your industry at what you do?

THE 25 CORE NEEDS OF *FIX THIS NEXT*

IMPACT

☐ 1 – **Transformation Orientation:** Does your business benefit clients through a transformation, beyond the transaction?

☐ 2 – **Mission Motivation:** Are all employees (including leadership) motivated more by delivering on the mission than by their individual roles?

☐ 3 – **Dream Alignment:** Are people's individual dreams aligned with the path of the business's grand vision?

☐ 4 – **Feedback Integrity:** Are your people, clients, and community empowered to give both critical and complimentary feedback?

☐ 5 – **Complementary Network:** Does your business seek to collaborate with vendors (including competitors) who serve the same customer base in order to improve the customer experience?

PROFIT

☐ 1 – **Debt Eradication:** Do your clients fervently defend, support, and help the business?

☐ 2 – **Intentional Leadership Turn:** Is there a plan for leadership to transition and stay fresh?

☐ 3 – **Heart-based Promoters:** Is the organization promoted by individuals inside and outside the organization, without need of direction?

☐ 4 – **Quarterly Dynamics:** Does your business have a clear vision for its future and dynamically adjust quarterly to make that vision become true?

☐ 5 – **Ongoing Adaptation:** Is the business designed to constantly adapt and improve, including finding ways to better and best itself?

DISCOVER MORE BOOKS

Want to spend less time working?

Want to make more money?

Want to be an industry leader?

Want to grow your business fast and strong?

Want to build your first company?

Available now at:

BARNES&NOBLE   **amazon**.com

mikemichalowicz.com

Want Mike to keynote your next event?

LET'S DO THIS!

Li Hayes • Speaking Coordinator for Mike Michalowicz

888-244-2843 x7008 • Li@MikeMichalowicz.com

MikeMichalowicz.com/Speaking

Mike Michalowicz works exclusively with GoLeeward.com, the leading speaking management firm. Hire Mike or other world class speakers by visiting GoLeeward.com. Finally! Your next event will benefit from professional speaker management, without any agency fees!

www.GoLeeward.com